HELPING THOSE WHO HURT

Books by

H. Norman Wright

FROM BETHANY HOUSE PUBLISHERS

The Complete Book of Christian Wedding Vows

Helping Those Who Hurt

The Perfect Catch

That's a Keeper

H. NORMAN WRIGHT

HELPING THOSE WHO HURT

BETHANYHOUSE

Helping Those Who Hurt: Reaching Out to Your Friends in Need
Copyright © 2003
H. Norman Wright

Cover design by Dan Thornberg

Published by Bethany House Publishers
11400 Hampshire Avenue South
Bloomington, Minnesota 55438
www.bethanyhouse.com

Bethany House Publishers is a Division of
Baker Book House Company, Grand Rapids, Michigan.

Printed in the United States of America

Library of Congress Cataloging-in-Publication Data

Wright, H. Norman.
    Helping those who hurt : reaching out to your friends in need / by H. Norman Wright.
       p. cm.
Includes bibliographical references (p.).
    ISBN 0-7642-2742-4 (pbk.)
    1. Helping behavior—Religious aspects—Christianity. 2. Friendship—Religious aspects—Christianity. I. Title.
    BV4647.H4W75   2003
    253—dc21
                                                  2003001456

CONTENTS

Chapter 1

CALLED TO HELP A FRIEND

IN ONE SMALL EUROPEAN VILLAGE was a town square that held a special statue. This statue was the pride and joy of the small town, but World War II arrived and soon the bombs began falling on the town. One day the statue was hit and blown to pieces. The residents collected all the shattered pieces and slowly did what they could to re-create it. When they finished the reconstruction of their beloved statue of Jesus, they noticed that the only pieces missing were the hands of Jesus. So they placed a plaque at the base of the statue with the words:

Now we are the only hands that Jesus has.

Isn't this our calling to those around us? We are His hands. You may have the desire to reach out and help your friends but hesitate. "What do I say? What do I do? What should I avoid?" You're not alone with your concern. You don't want to say or do the wrong thing and hurt your friends. And during a loss or crisis you can't rely on them to tell you what they need. They may not know or have the energy it takes to tell you.

What will you say when a friend comes to you and says:

"I've just been told I have cancer and it's terminal."

"It was a phone call . . . he's dead . . . he's been killed . . . my husband."

"My daughter just told me she's been molested for three years."

"I was in the video store and it was robbed! The gun went off. I can't even think."

"I went to school to pick up my son. He wasn't there. They say he was kidnapped."

"My husband just told me he wants a divorce. I'm shocked. I didn't know anything was wrong."

I was sitting at the kitchen table in my daughter's home looking through a magazine while Sheryl fed her six-month-old daughter. The phone rang and she answered the call while continuing to feed her daughter. When she said, "Oh, no. I'm so sorry to hear that. That must have been a shock," my ears perked up. I continued to listen and watch her facial expressions. It was apparent that her friend was in some kind of distress. I observed Sheryl while she listened and reflected back what she was hearing. She made statements like, "So, you found the evidence and that's what led you to confront him," and "You're sounding hurt and disappointed." From time to time she asked questions: "Which of the children are aware of this?" and "How will _____ handle this at her stage in life?" She also asked, "Had you thought about this possibility?" and "Have you considered this?"

When her friend wasn't sure or seemed to waiver Sheryl said, "Is that really your responsibility at this time or is it his?" She helped her friend reconsider what was best to do and encouraged her to take the necessary steps. "You've given him more than a chance and trusted his word. Now it's been broken. I think you'll know what to do." She helped her friend explore several options as well as the consequences. On several occasions she reflected and clarified while her friend was thinking out loud. I could tell just from my daughter's comments and facial expressions that her friend was fairly devastated. I thought it was good that this woman had a trusted friend to talk with and help her work through this life-changing event.

My daughter wasn't judgmental in any way, but assisted her to clarify the problem. Her friend needed support, someone to listen, to help her sort through the options, and to help her stabilize her life at that time. After Sheryl hung up the phone we talked for a while. Sheryl made the comment, "I'm sure glad I'm not a counselor. I wouldn't want to do this for a living." I just looked at her, smiled, and said, "Oh, sure. You've only done this for fifteen years as a manicurist. You've helped as many women as some counselors have while you were sitting there doing their nails." She laughed because it was true. She helped many who would never go to talk to a counselor or pastor. But they would listen to her because of some of her own life experiences, her listening, her insight, and her desire to help. And so can you.

After forty years of counseling I'm convinced that as many as one-third to one-half of all the people I've seen didn't need to come and see me. That is—they didn't need to see me if they had a trained pastor, lay caregiver, or knowledgeable friend to meet with. I'm all for professional counseling when it's needed, but many issues can be resolved with the help of a friend who is willing to learn how to minister to others. And as Christians it is not an option to help or not help others. That is what the Christian life is all about—ministering to others. Many back off from this because they don't know what to say or do. That's understandable and acceptable. I still find myself in that position from time to time. And when that happens I go to work and learn what I need.

If you are saying, "I wouldn't know what to say or what to do," there is a solution. You *can* listen. Everyone can. It's not that difficult. Just imagine what our churches would be like if people knew what to say and do as well as what *not* to say and do! This can happen. This needs to happen. If others have no one to help them, no one to talk with, they end up talking to themselves. And the advice and help they give themselves isn't the best.

Many years ago (more than I'd like to admit) I was on the staff of a church as minister of education and youth. A man by the name of Alan Loy McGinnis was attending our church while completing his graduate work. Since he was also a minister, he would preach from time to time in the evening service. One Sunday night he walked up to the pulpit and said, "Tonight I would like to share with you what to say, what not to say, what to do, and what not to do at a time of bereavement."

Ours was not a note-taking congregation, until that moment. As I sat on the platform I could see people reaching for offering envelopes, prayer request cards, or any other piece of paper they could find to write on. I still have my notes from that evening. It was the first (and unfortunately the last) time I've ever heard a message on how to help another person at a time of need. Those in attendance that evening left with a greater sense of confidence on how to help another person.

You'll be more likely to reach out if you know what to say.

It's true—helping a hurting person *is* a bit scary. We want to do the right thing, not do the wrong thing, say what will help, not say what will hurt, and all these thoughts could be going on simultaneously. To add to our confusion, our friend is "not quite herself." She's different. We want our friend fixed, back to normal.

All you have to do is care. Harold Ivan Smith described the process so well:

> Grief sharers always look for an opportunity to actively care. You can never "fix" an individual's grief, but you can wash the sink full of dishes, listen to him or her talk, take his or her kids to the park. You can never "fix" an individual's grief but you can visit the cemetery with him or her.
>
> Grief sharing is not about fixing—it's about showing up. Coming alongside. Being interruptible. "Hanging out" with the bereaving. In the words of World War II veterans, "present and reporting for duty."

The grief path is not a brief path. It's a marathon, not a sprint.[1]

What can you expect from a friend who is hurting? Actually, not very much. And the more her experience moves beyond a loss and closer to a crisis or trauma, the more this is true. Sometimes you'll see a friend experiencing a case of the "crazies." Her response seems irrational. She's not herself. Her behavior is different from or even abnormal compared to the person not going through a major loss. Just remember she's reacting to an out-of-the-ordinary event. What she *experienced* is abnormal, so her *response* is actually quite normal. If what the person has experienced is traumatic she may even seem to exhibit some of the symptoms of ADD (Attention Deficit Disorder). And because your friend is this way she is *not* to be avoided. Others are needed at this time. These are responses you *can* expect. Your friend is no longer functioning as she once did—and probably won't for a while.

YOU ARE NEEDED

When a person experiences a sudden intrusion in her life, a disruption, you are needed. If you (or another friend) aren't available, the only person she has to talk with for guidance, support, and direction is herself. And who wants support from someone struggling with a case of the "crazies"?

You are needed. But a problem may arise when your friend doesn't realize that she needs you, or at least that she needs you but not at that *particular time*. Your sensitivity is needed at this point. Remember when your friend is hurting and facing a loss, you too are dealing with a loss. The relationship you had with your friend has changed. It's not the same. It's no longer equal. You may feel as though you're the giver and your friend is the taker. Your relationship is off balance. The sharing the two of you had before has changed. The give-and-take you used to experience has vanished. What's important to you does not seem important to your friend. Your life and experiences have taken a backseat to the experience of your friend.

You can't put a time limit on your role as a helper or giver. This may get old for you, especially when it stretches on for months. Remember that when your relationship gets back to normal, it will be a new normal. It won't be the same. Sometimes a hurting friend ends up feeling resentful over being dependent upon you while at the same time appreciating all you've done for her.

> Your friend in mourning—though he doesn't perceive himself that way—is self-centered. You simply cannot exist for him as a whole person, probably for a very long time. This can be hard on relationships. Friends get weary of ceasing to be perceived as human beings with feelings and problems and hopes in their own right. They get weary of being there for the other person in seemingly a one-sided relationship. But suffice it to say that your friend in mourning will not be able to empathize with you about things involving you for many months—or maybe years.[2]

WHAT CAN YOU DO?

You can listen even when she's not talking. Sometimes she's not able to talk. But your attentive presence lets your friend know you're there to listen. You let her know you want to hear her story when she's up to talking about it.

If your friend is devastated and coming apart at the seams or sitting there stunned, you can't make her feel better or fix her. When we try it's often to help us feel useful and relieve our anxiety of seeing someone in this state. Remember, you can never be all you want to be or all your friend wants you to be for her.[3]

What else can you expect? The world your friend experiences now won't be your world. Often she will retreat into her world and not let you in. Because of what she is going through your activities may not seem as significant as they once did. You will reevaluate your own standards and values. Your family may see how your friend's problems are changing you and pressure you to back off. They want *you* back to normal too.

You will be hurt at times since some of what you offer or do will be rejected. Because you haven't experienced the same loss, she may feel uncomfortable with you while at the same time want your help. Remember your friend is not functioning normally. In your heart and mind give her permission not to be as she was. If something is said or done that offends you, remind yourself that your friend cannot be expected to be as she was. You may wonder, *Did I say something wrong? Am I off base?* The answer is no. You're dealing with unpredictability. You're all right.

You may be tempted at times to set your friend straight spiritually. You might hear statements like, "I thought I could count on God but even He let me down" or "How could a loving God let something like that happen?" or "I think I'm losing my faith in God. I can't even pray anymore." Squelch your desire to start quoting Bible verses, shove a book in her face, or try to give answers. Be glad you're hearing where she is spiritually. Respond with a simple "Yes, what's happened doesn't make much sense, does it? It's hard to understand. I wish I had an answer for you," or just listen and reflect.

There will be times when your friend doesn't want you around. If you sense that might be the case, ask her, "What would be more comfortable for you at this time, for me to be here with you or to give you some space? I can do either." If your presence isn't needed, say, "I'll check back with you another time to see what I can do to assist you."

Let your friend know that you won't be offended if she doesn't want you to be there. And since none of us are mind readers, there will be times when you don't have any idea of what she needs. Let her know it's all right for her to tell you specifically what she needs, even if it's to say, "I don't know."

I will make this statement several times in this book: The best support you can give your friend is to *normalize her feelings*. This simply means reassuring her that what she is experiencing is natural; she isn't crazy. This advice can provide the greatest relief of all. But it means *you* need to understand what someone experiences from a loss or a trauma. (This will be discussed in chapter 7.)

BIBLICAL GUIDELINES FOR HELPING

How can you help a friend? There are many elements involved. In Proverbs 3:5–6 we are instructed to "Lean on, trust in, and be confident in the Lord with all your heart and mind and do not rely on your own insight or understanding. In all your ways know, recognize, and acknowledge Him, and he will direct and make straight and plain your paths" (AMP).

A similar thought is in Proverbs 15:28: "The mind of the [uncompromisingly] righteous studies how to answer, but the mouth of the wicked pours out evil things" (AMP). With all their years of training and experience, professional counselors frequently wonder what they should do or say. This experience prompts all of us to go back to the Lord and ask, "Lord, what should I do now? What does this person need?" You'll find yourself there time and time again. If you begin to assist and help your friend out of your own strength, mistakes will be made. We all need to rely upon the power and wisdom of God.

Helping others includes experiencing genuine interest and love for the individual. We can listen and rely upon the power of God for knowing how to respond, but we must also have a genuine interest and love. If it's not there you can't fake it, and your friend will know if you are. Proverbs 27:9: "Oil and perfume rejoice the heart; so does the sweetness of a friend's counsel that comes from the heart" (AMP). It's so easy to "flip off" an answer that's superficial and doesn't meet your friend's need. If it doesn't deal with the problem, she will be disappointed. We have to ask ourselves, "How do I really feel about this individual who is coming to me? Am I genuinely concerned? If not, maybe I should pray about my own attitude. Perhaps I'm not the one to try to help." You will be drawn to help some you know and not others. It could be their problems are beyond you, overwhelm you, or activate some unresolved issues in your own life.

To help someone else, you need to know when to speak and when enough has been said. Proverbs 10:19 emphasizes this principle: "In a multitude of words transgression is not lacking, but he who restrains his lips is prudent" (AMP). The Living Bible is very graphic: "Don't talk so much. You keep putting your foot in your mouth. Be sensible and turn off the flow!" Proverbs 11:12: "He who belittles and despises his neighbor lacks sense, but a man of understanding keeps silent" (AMP). Proverbs 17:27: "The smart person says very little, and one with understanding stays calm" (NCV). This is a sign of an individual who has knowledge. He chooses his words well. "Even fools seem to be wise if they keep quiet; if they don't speak, they appear to understand" (17:28 NCV).

Proverbs 29:20: "Do you see a man who is hasty in his words? There is more hope for a [self-confident] fool than for him" (AMP). Being hasty means you just go ahead and blurt out what you're thinking without considering the consequences, without considering the effect it will have on others. If you're an extrovert, you probably need to talk to think something through. Extroverts tend to talk first and then realize what they've said. This is a time to hold back and get your thoughts in order. When you are ministering to a hurting friend and she shares something that shocks you, don't feel that you have to respond immediately. I've heard people say, "You did *what?*" Take a few moments to pray, asking God to give you the words. Then try to formulate what you want to say.

If you don't know what to say, one of the best things to do is ask for more information: "Tell me some more about it" or "Give me some more background." This gives you more time. You don't have to come right out and say something. There may be times when you say, "I need a few seconds to go through what you said and decide what to share at this time." This takes the pressure off you and also off your friend.

Timing is yet another principle. Proverbs 15:23: "A man has joy in making an apt answer, and a word spoken at the right moment— how good it is!" (AMP). The correct answer spoken at the right moment is needed.

Keeping confidences is foundational. Can you keep a confidence when somebody shares something with you? Proverbs 11:13: "Gossips can't keep secrets, but a trustworthy person can" (NCV). Proverbs 20:19: "Gossips can't keep secrets, so avoid people who talk too much" (NCV). If you have a friend who is a gossiper, who can't keep something hidden, the scripture is saying, Watch out! Don't associate with that person too much. Proverbs 21:23: "He who guards his mouth and his tongue keeps himself from troubles" (AMP).

Undoubtedly most of us, when we have had something shared with us, have had the temptation to share it with others. Even a confidence from a friend. And the more shocking it is, the more we're tempted to share. Some respond with, "Wait until you hear what I heard this week." People love to use that as a vehicle to conversation with somebody else. But such conversation is a violation of trust and a violation of friendship, and tremendous damage is done. What we must do as a Christian and as a friend is ask God to help us bury confidential information deep inside or give it away to the Lord so that it will not come out on purpose or through some unconscious motivation. Does your friend want you to share this issue with anyone else including family? Ask her. (If she's highly suicidal or homicidal you will have to get some assistance.)

Another passage reflects the idea of understanding. Proverbs

25:20: "Singing songs to someone who is sad is like taking away his coat on a cold day or pouring vinegar on soda" (NCV). Being merry, joyful, happy around the person who is deeply hurting and suffering, making inappropriate comments or jokes, or even statements such as, "Oh, you really don't feel that way, snap out of it," is inappropriate. Your friend hurts so much she's unable to focus on what is happening. Inappropriate statements or jokes can be very, very painful to the person who has experienced a loss or is traumatized.

So how do you give good advice? It's possible to receive wrong advice. In fact, probably on many occasions all of us have struggled and friends have given us advice. But it may not have been what we needed at that time. In fact, it's possible that we could have received five different viewpoints if we asked five different people, then were left wondering, *What in the world do I do now? Whom do I believe?*

If you give suggestions, give tentative ones. "What if you did. . . ?" "Have you ever considered. . . ?" "What possibilities have you come up with?" A safety factor we can employ if we are going to give advice is to give several alternatives. Don't say to a person, "This is exactly what you need to do." If you do, you are assuming the responsibility for the solution and if your suggestion doesn't work, she may come back and say, "You really gave me a stupid idea. It didn't work. It's your fault." Giving several tentative suggestions not only is safer for you, but causes the friend to think it through. Most people have the ability to resolve their problems, but they need the encouragement to do it.

One of the ways of helping a friend is a gentle confrontation when you see her heading down the wrong path. Confrontation is not an attack on another person; she may already be feeling guilty and ashamed, and to experience judgment or condemnation rather than a gentle nudge is nothing less than rejection.

Confronting another person can only come when you experience empathy for her. A confrontation should be an act of grace. It's done to reveal discrepancies or distortions in someone's intended direction or thinking. Confrontation is also used to challenge the under-developed and the unused skills and resources of your friend.

Your purpose in confronting your friend should be to help her make better decisions for herself, become more accepting of where she is in life, and to be less destructive and more productive. "Wounds from a friend can be trusted, but an enemy multiplies kisses" (Proverbs 27:6). "A rebuke impresses a man of discernment more than a hundred lashes a fool" (Proverbs 17:10).

But you cannot use the same approach for every person; you must be sensitive to her needs. Adaptability is important. "And we earnestly beseech you, brethren, admonish (warn and seriously advise) those who are out of line . . . , encourage the timid and fainthearted, help and give your support to the weak souls, [and] be very patient with everybody [always keeping your temper]" (1 Thessalonians 5:14 AMP).

How do you confront? Not with anger or with a statement. You may want to point out that what someone's doing is irresponsible or even dumb, but you'll offend and even sever the relationship. Your friend needs to hear care and concern in your voice; confrontation can be made in a tentative manner with statements such as, "I wonder if . . ." "Could it be. . . ?" "Is it possible. . . ?" "Does this make sense to you?" and "How do you react to this perception?" With your questions, lead her to where you want her to go. Practice these questions out loud again and again until they're a part of your helping reservoir of information and approach.

Another principle we find in the Word of God is helping and edifying. Some of these passages might be familiar to you. Galatians 6:2 teaches the concept of bearing one another's burdens. Romans 14:19 reads, "So let us then definitely aim for and eagerly pursue what makes for harmony and for mutual upbuilding (edification and development) of one another" (AMP). The word *edify*, which is part of helping, means to hold up or to promote growth in Christian wisdom, grace, virtue, and holiness. Our helping includes edification. Helping means assisting a person to do something for her betterment. We have to ask ourselves, "Is what I'm sharing with that person going to cause her to grow in the Christian life and assist her to be strong?" A friend might come to you and say, "I really want you to help me." What does she mean by *help*? She might mean agreeing with her point of view, or even taking her side. That is where you get into difficulty—taking sides.

Another way of helping others is encouragement. Proverbs 12:25: "Anxiety in a man's heart weighs it down, but an encouraging word makes it glad" (AMP). First Thessalonians 5:11: "Therefore encourage (admonish, exhort) one another and edify (strengthen and build up) one another, just as you are doing" (AMP).

The *American Heritage Dictionary* has one of the better definitions of *encourage*. It's a "tendency or disposition to expect the best possible outcome, or to dwell on the most hopeful aspect of a situation." When this is your attitude or perspective, you'll be able to encourage others. Encouragement is "to inspire; to continue on a chosen course; to impart courage or confidence."

Encouragement is recognizing the other person as having worth and dignity. It means paying attention to her when she is sharing with you. It's listening to her in a way that lets her know she's being listened to.

In Acts 18:27, the word *encourage* means "to urge forward or persuade." In 1 Thessalonians 5:11 it means to stimulate another person to the ordinary duties of life.

Scripture uses a variety of words to describe both our involvement with others as well as the actual relationship. *Urge* (*parakaleo*) means "to beseech or exhort." It is intended to create an environment of urgency to listen and respond to a directive. It is a mildly active verb. Paul used it in Romans 12:1 and in 1 Corinthians 1:4.

The word encourage (*paramutheomai*) means "to console, comfort, and cheer up." This process includes elements of understanding, redirecting of thoughts, and a general shifting of focus from the negative to the positive. In the context of the verse, it refers to the timid ("fainthearted," in the King James Version) individual who is discouraged and ready to give up. It's a matter of loaning your faith and hope to the person until her own develops.

Help (*anechomai*) primarily consists of taking interest in, being devoted to, rendering assistance, or holding up spiritually and emotionally. It is not so much an active involvement as a passive approach. It suggests the idea of coming alongside a person and supporting her. In the context of 1 Thessalonians 5:14, it seems to refer to those who are incapable of helping themselves.

Hebrews 3:13 says we're to "encourage one another daily." In the setting of this verse, encouragement is associated with protecting the believer from callousness.

Hebrews 10:25 says, "Let us encourage one another." This time the word means to keep someone on her feet who, if left to herself, would collapse. Your encouragement serves like the concrete pilings of a structural support.

Involvement and empathy are the scriptural basis for helping. Empathy is one of the most important commodities for helping. It's viewing the situation through your friend's eyes, feeling as she feels. The scriptural admonition to bear one another's burdens in Galatians 6:2 and to rejoice with those who rejoice and weep with those who weep in Romans 12:15 is what we call empathy.

It involves discrimination—to be able to get inside the other person, to look at the world through her perspective or frame of reference, and to get a feeling for what her world is like. Not only is it the ability to discriminate, but also to communicate to your friend this understanding in such a manner that she realizes you have picked up her feelings and behavior. We must be able to see with her eyes what her world is like. It is like being able to see another person's joy, to understand what underlies that joy, and to communicate this understanding to the person. Can you do this? Yes, you can learn. Be patient with yourself and with others.

Be open to God's leading at this time. May the words of a man who gave his life for others on 9/11 guide you:

> Lord, take me where You want me to go,
> Let me meet whom You want me to meet.
> Help me to say what You want me to say.
> And keep me from getting in Your way!
> —Father Mychal Judge[4]

Chapter 2

THE MISERABLE COMFORTERS IN YOUR FRIEND'S LIFE

IF AN ENEMY WERE INSULTING ME, I could endure it; if a foe were raising himself against me, I could hide from him. But it is you, a man like myself, my companion, my close friend, with whom I once enjoyed sweet fellowship as we walked with the throng at the house of God" (Psalm 55:12–14).

"Even my close friend, whom I trusted, he who shared my bread, has lifted up his heel against me" (Psalm 41:9).

There is one additional source of pain your friend will need to contend with—other people who make statements that hurt rather than console, hinder rather than comfort, and prolong the pain rather than relieve it. These people are secondary wounders. They'll give unwanted and bad advice as well as improperly applied Scripture. They're all around, even at church, and your friend won't be the first to experience this. Remember Job?

> [Job] had four well-meaning but insufferable friends who came over to cheer him up and try to explain [his suffering]. They said that anybody with enough sense to come in out of the rain knew that God was just. They said that anybody old enough to spell his own name knew that since God was just, he made bad

things happen to bad people and good things happen to good people. They said that such being the case, you didn't need a Harvard diploma to figure out that since bad things had happened to Job, then *ipso facto* he must have done something bad himself. But Job hadn't, and he said so, and that's not all he said either. "Worthless physicians are you all," he said. "Oh that you would keep silent, and it would be your wisdom" (Job 13:4–5). They were a bunch of theological quacks, in other words, and the smartest thing they could do was shut up. But they were too busy explaining things to listen.[1]

WORDS BETTER LEFT UNSAID

Expect people to make statements that your friend would rather not hear. It will be difficult for her to respond to these people the way she would like to because of her state of grief or trauma. Perhaps others would learn not to make such insensitive statements if someone spoke up and said, "That's not true and it's not helpful. If you want to be helpful I would appreciate it if you would . . ." But sometimes we excuse what these people say as well meaning, which is questionable. Oftentimes they're just reflecting their own anxieties, fears, or lack of having dealt with issues in their own lives. Remember, this is not advice coming from experts!

Let your friend know she can anticipate at least three common reactions from the people she confides in.

The Inability of Others to Accept the Bad News

There are numerous reasons for the inability to accept bad news, but the results are the same: People can't handle the situation or accept the person who has created the problem.

Often people will verbalize sympathy and support, but their attitude and behavior communicates rejection. Your hurting friend will wonder which message to believe. On one hand, she'll feel them reaching out to her, but on the other, they're pulling away.

Remind her that when other people are uncomfortable with a situation, they're feeling and, by their nonverbal responses, saying, "I want you 'normal' as soon as possible, or at least I want you to act that way." But your friend can't and won't be "normal" for some time, and no one else can determine how she should respond. This is her situation; she's upset over her tragedy and loss. No one should rob her of her feelings and grief. I read a statement once that describes death, but it applies to other situations as well: "When a person is born we celebrate; when they marry we jubilate; but when they die we act as if nothing has happened."[2]

The more others hear about your friend's difficulties, the greater the level of their discomfort, and they don't want her discomfort invading their lives. So they may distance themselves. I've seen situations in which the spouse, parents, or the children were no longer invited to their friends' homes, as though what they were experiencing might somehow be contagious.

When people react badly to your friend, it may help to explain some of the adjustments they are experiencing. The person who is hurting could tell others she understands how uncomfortable they may feel learning about this. Don't expect them to open up and say they're having difficulty with the situation. They probably won't. But if she admits her struggle with her mixture of feelings, at least others may feel more comfortable with her, whether they admit anything or not.

Unsolicited Advice

Everyone is an expert or knows of a similar case, and since those who care want to help, they give emphatic suggestions about steps that should be taken. Sometimes they're offended if your friend doesn't show enthusiasm and indicate she's going to follow their advice immediately. Too often, however, their suggestions are contrary to a selected plan or the advice of a counselor.

Your friend can thank them for their concern and suggestions and let them know they are adding to the wealth of information she's been gathering, but she shouldn't commit to taking their advice. There will likely be times when nothing is working, the experts don't know what to do, or she's in a state of panic, and she may find herself jumping from one piece of advice to another. Soon she'll be overwhelmed by a lack of follow-through on any of the suggestions. Before she takes any suggestions, she needs to reflect on them. If she's still in a state of shock or crisis, let a few trusted friends help make decisions.

Sometimes it's not just advice she has to contend with, but also the third degree. You've probably heard the questions before: "Has this happened before in your family?" "Do you have a good lawyer?"

Overwhelmed With Help

Yet another reaction, especially from people who really care, will be to overwhelm your friend with help. I've seen relatives and friends invade a family's boundaries and actually take away their decision-making opportunities. Your friend needs help in determining how much assistance she wants and establishing boundaries with any intrusive friends or relatives. Most people won't have any idea what she needs or doesn't need until your friend outlines it for them. They'll want to help, which is fine, but only your friend can determine the type and quantity of help she needs. Remind her it's perfectly all right for her to be in charge of her decisions.

A good starting point for your friend is to make a list of her needs and questions and then list the type of outside help she's looking for. It's all right to take time to think, to pray and consider the options and the consequences of each. She doesn't need to let others pressure or rush her into anything.[3]

WHAT NOT TO SAY

Listen to these firsthand experiences of being wounded by others:

My first day back to work after my mother's funeral, a

coworker said, "I know just how you feel. My cat died recently." How could someone compare my mother's major role in my life with a cat? It would have been more sensitive to simply say, "I'm sorry."[4]

Our young daughter, who was dying from leukemia, loved to read. When we took her to the ophthalmologist for a new pair of glasses, he said, "She's going to die soon anyway. Don't waste your money on a new prescription." He didn't understand that dying children need to make every day count and live to the fullest the life they have left.[5]

My son, who had Down's syndrome, died when he was twenty years old. A relative said, "What a blessing. He is better off now." I wondered if her twenty-two-year-old son would be "better off" if he were dead and if that would bless her. Does an IQ make one life worth more than another? Does an IQ change a mother's grief? I had cared for my precious, loving son his entire life, and I desperately missed him and his daily hugs. Many thought I would be relieved. Very few people understood my loss and I felt very alone in my grieving.[6]

Following my miscarriage people would say, "At least you have other children" or "God probably took the baby because there was something wrong with it" or "At least you are healthy and will probably conceive again." After my grandfather died, my grandmother told me that friends said, "At least you had all those years together." Don't say AT LEAST. Don't try to minimize someone's pain. It only insults the griever.[7]

When my wife died, an acquaintance said, "God must have needed another angel in heaven, another flower in his garden." It is not comforting to have God reduced to a selfish, needy deity who must take from us. He is God.[8]

I waited for days, even weeks, before I could bring myself to tell anyone about our child. I used to think it wasn't because I was ashamed or embarrassed or anything, but I guess I did have those feelings. I don't know why I felt that way. Maybe I felt John's rebellion was my fault, even thought I knew it wasn't. It couldn't be. I guess I was afraid of their reaction. You never know what you're going to hear. I didn't want their advice. They're not experts, and I didn't want them telling me we were bad parents.

Not only will there be comments that hurt but responses such as withdrawing. Your friend may wonder if she's contracted the plague. One insightful individual said:

You feel so isolated within yourself. When people withdraw from you because of their own discomfort, in a way, it's almost like an accusation that you were at fault. You feel you *must* have done something wrong, or this wouldn't be happening to you. On the other hand, you almost feel like they don't want to be around you because they feel it might be catching. I know people don't know what to say. I would rather they'd come and be with me or ask permission, "Would you like someone to be with you?" rather than feel, "Well, I don't know what to say so I think I'll stay away."

Perhaps you've experienced this yourself. If so, you know the pain a friend may be experiencing. We call it rejection.

Over the years I've heard so many inappropriate remarks that intensify the hurt and grief. I shudder over some of these insensitive remarks. And yes, sometimes I react in anger over comments that I can't believe anyone would make. It could be it's not just a friend but you who have been on the receiving end of such comments over the years. The examples in this chapter are given as a guide of what *not* to say. I wish every church would give these wounding comments to every person in the congregation along with what *to* say (which will be in a later chapter). What a difference this could make!

Here is what I've heard over the years:

"I don't understand why you're still crying. Life goes on, you know."

"Look, you only lost your stepfather. What about your mother? She has a greater loss than you and she's pulled herself together."

"No one should feel that way about losing a cat. It's only an animal. You had it for ten years and you can find another one."

"This will make your family closer. It's an opportunity to grow together."

"I'm sure this will teach the other college students to be more diligent in their studies."

"Don't you appreciate what you have left?"

"Next time we'll be sure not to use that doctor or hospital."

"You've started out in new jobs before, so just look at this layoff as a great opportunity like George did when he got fired."

"Be brave."

"You shouldn't feel that way. After all, you have the Lord."

"It's time to pull yourself together. You wouldn't want Mother seeing you that way, would you?"

"The past needs to be put behind us. Let's move on to the future with God."

"At least he didn't suffer."

"Well, just be glad it wasn't your only child."

"Look at it this way. Losing your husband this young and without children will make it easier for you to handle."

"Everyone dies sooner or later. He just died sooner."

"The children need you to be strong."

"If you had had a burglar alarm in your house, this never would have happened."

"This must be God's will."

Statements like these don't help or comfort. They only intensify the person's feelings of loss and despair.

Sometimes people take an "It could have been worse" approach to their grieving friend in the hope of lessening the hurt. Unfortunately, at this point in time it doesn't work. In *The Survival Guide for Widows*, the author describes this approach:

> I have one friend who, whenever we got together, at one point would nod her head wisely and say sententiously, "There are worse things than death." It was home-truth time, and she wanted me to know how lucky I was that I didn't have a living vegetable tied up to tubes in the hospital, or a human skeleton wasting away with pain in front of my eyes. I know, I know. We are given enough strength, I hope, to bear our own pain. I would not trade with others, nor they with me, in all likelihood. . . . But the widow doesn't feel very lucky and resents being reminded that she still owes a debt of gratitude. She'll come around to it.[9]

In her dramatic and sensitively written book, *The Fire That Will Not Die*, Michele McBride gives numerous accounts of the thoughtless, sometimes devastating, comments people made that added to her severe physical and psychological pain.

> It was embarrassing for me and my friends when a stranger stopped me on the street to ask what happened to my face. This startled all of us, and everyone felt bad—and I never knew exactly what to say. People were crude and said things like "Are you contagious?" and "Should you be out in public?" Once someone told me I should stay home and not frighten people on the streets. I tried to force myself into believing these people did not mean to be cruel. . . .
>
> Another time I was in a store with my girl friend and we stood paralyzed in horror as a man grabbed the scarf off my head to display my facial scars to another person. The hurt I was experiencing from these onslaughts was worse than all the pain I

endured in the hospital when all the bandages were pulled off my body.[10]

Julie Breuninger, founder of Face to Face, a support group for parents of children with craniofacial disfigurements, relates her experiences. Julie's son, Jonathan, has Crouzon syndrome, a malformation of the skull and face caused by premature closure of the skull's suture lines. "Our society places so much value on beauty that people just couldn't accept Jonathan. We would go to McDonald's and kids would ask why he looked so funny or parents would look away. When they'd hear him talk, they'd act surprised. They assumed he was retarded."[11]

Why do we react this way? How should we react? Again, the answers come from those who know best: the persons who are disfigured. In a newsletter article published by the Phoenix Society, a national organization providing self-help services to burn survivors and their families, these answers were given by Alan Breslau:

> It is perfectly normal to be alarmed at something or someone who looks out of the ordinary because it or they might present a threat. . . . The disfigured person is going to be cautiously examined to ascertain if there is any threat being presented. The other reason is that no one has taught us how to deal with people who are disfigured. When a child stares and the mother says, "Don't look at him like that!" she is giving the wrong message. Not noticing disfigurement is as bad as staring, because if the disfigurement is obvious, then by looking away you are sending the message: "discomfort."
>
> As a disfigured person, I feel much more comfortable when people are direct and ask, "What happened to you?" By facing the reality, I can satisfy their curiosity, put them at ease, and probably make a friend. To the mother with the little child, I confront her and say, "It's all right for her to look because I do look different, and it is normal to be curious." Then I tell them both how it happened. Now I have two new friends.[12]

If we had some way of telling everyone how to deal with the disfigured, neither party would then feel uncomfortable.

A mother who lost her child shared her painful experience:

> All too common were the reminders. "You can have other babies," as if this baby were replaceable. "Don't get pregnant too soon. You don't want to replace this baby." Then they would add, "But be glad you can have others."
>
> People say things to console themselves. There is no need to try to say things to make you feel better because *there is not a thing they can say—not a word, not a phrase—that will make you feel better about your loss.*

Her last statement is full of insight and wisdom. You can't take your friend's pain away. You can't fix others. Neither can I. None of us is the Great Healer.

Erin Linn compiled and categorized the painful and glib clichés that are thrown about so easily:

"Be Strong" Clichés

Big boys don't cry.

The children are flexible . . . they will bounce back.

You must be strong for the children.

Support groups are for wimps.

You've just got to get a hold of yourself!

Others have held up well. You can too.

Cheer up.

No sense crying over spilled milk.

This is nature's way.

"Hurry Up" Clichés

You're not your old self.

Out of sight, out of mind.

Time will heal.

You're young, and you will be able to make a new life for yourself.

I just don't understand your behavior.

Life goes on.

No sense dwelling on the past.

"Guilt" Clichés

If you look around, you can always find someone who is worse off than yourself.

This is the work of the devil (which means that if you had a closer relationship with God, the devil could not have had his way).

If I were you, I would do it this way.

Count your blessings.

Only the good die young.

If you had been a better Christian, this would not have happened to you.

Think of all your precious memories.

It's a blessing.

"God" Clichés

God needs him more than you do.

He is happy now, because he's with God.

God did this to show how powerful He can be in your life.

It was God's will.

God never gives us more than we can handle.

God helps those who help themselves.

"Discount" Clichés

I know just how you feel.

Silence is golden.

If there is anything I can do, just call me.

You can have more children.

It's better to have loved and lost than never to have loved at all.

Be glad you don't have a problem like mine.

What you don't know, won't hurt you.[13]

THE EXTENT OF PAIN

How would David have responded to such comments? The extent of your friend's pain is probably reflected in David's words.

> Be merciful to me, Lord, for I am faint;
> O Lord, heal me, for my bones are in agony.
> My soul is in anguish.
> How long, O Lord, how long?
>
> Turn, O Lord, and deliver me;
> save me because of your unfailing love.
> No one remembers you when he is dead.
> Who praises you from the grave?
>
> I am worn out from groaning;
> all night long I flood my bed with weeping
> and drench my couch with my tears.
> My eyes grow weak with sorrow.
>   (Psalm 6:2–7)

What would you have said to David? How would you have comforted him?

What makes it so bad is that some of the worst comments come from well-intentioned acquaintances. A mother once said: "Someone told me it's probably a good thing she did die, so she wouldn't suffer. It tore me up for someone to say it was a good thing for a child to die. They haven't been there themselves. Another said, 'Maybe it's a good thing she died, because when she got older, she might have gotten into all kinds of trouble.' "

Statements of this nature merely added to the existing pain.

An all-too-common remark made to parents of children with cancer or a mentally handicapped child is, "You must be a special person, and God must really love you to give you a child like this."

Is this what a parent feels? As one mother said, "I'm not special;

I don't want to do this either. In essence she's saying, 'God would never pick me for such things because I'm not strong.' I'm not that strong. And if I were, I'd rather my child was well or normal."

And then you get the medical "experts," who give unsolicited advice about chemotherapy. They'll say, "I wouldn't give her that stuff; people die from that." Parents struggle making decisions anyway—it's an overwhelming responsibility. But then you have people who don't know anything about it question you. Parents would rather hear, "What helped you come to that decision?" or "That must have been a hard decision to make."

One of the best ways I've discovered to help someone explain her situation and her needs is to write and photocopy a letter she can give to relatives, friends, acquaintances, and anyone else who asks. The letter states what has happened, what it will be like for her and her family, what others can expect, and what they can do for the person. By doing this, some of the pain is lessened by not having to tell the same story over and over—sometimes the repetition intensifies the pain.

Here's an example of a family in crisis:

Dear Friend,

You may have heard that we've had some difficulty with our oldest daughter. This has been very hard for my husband and me, and sometimes we're embarrassed over what has happened. Who would have expected that she would use drugs, leave high school, and live on the streets? The reason for this letter is that it's too painful to have to explain this over and over and over to our friends and relatives. We wish the problem would go away or we could just hide. But it doesn't and we can't, and we don't have any idea how this is going to turn out or when it will be over.

Please just keep asking how we're doing and continue to pray for us. We probably won't be the same each time you talk with us. We could be angry one time or depressed and dejected another time. Help us to talk, and just listen. If you have some suggestions, we will consider them, and perhaps something you say will benefit us.

You may find yourself with many questions as well as feelings too. You may be shocked and find yourself angry, wishing you could talk to our daughter and knock some sense into her head. You may even wonder, as we did, where we went wrong. What could we have done differently so this would not have happened? If you hear anyone judging us, please let them know we are already doing this and need their understanding.

Please don't withdraw from us. We need your support more than ever. Pray for us as well as our daughter. We want to continue to love her, encourage her, and believe in her. Pray that we won't just concentrate on our hurt but on her needs as well. Don't be surprised if we call you from time to time and say we need to talk, or ask you to go to dinner and talk about anything other than our daughter, since we need a break.

This is a loss to us and to our other children, and it's painful.

Thank you for your support.

When your friend can take a positive, assertive step in reaching out to others and letting them know what she needs, she'll gain confidence and strength. She will feel less like a victim. Above all, she needs to talk about her feelings and concerns with family members. Encourage her not to try to protect them from the news, no matter what the problem, and to be aware of the danger of neglecting them because of all the attention given to the problem person.

Perhaps the words and advice of a hurting person summarize what's best not to do and what to do:

PLEASE

PLEASE, don't ask me if I'm over it yet.
I'll never be over it.

PLEASE, don't tell me she's in a better place.
She isn't here with me.

PLEASE, don't say at least she isn't suffering.
I haven't come to terms with why she had to suffer at all.

PLEASE, don't tell me you know how I feel
unless you have lost a child.

PLEASE, don't ask me if I feel better.
Bereavement isn't a condition that clears up.

PLEASE, don't tell me at least you had her for so many years.
What year would you choose for your child to die?

PLEASE, don't tell me God never gives us more than we can bear.

PLEASE, just say you are sorry.

PLEASE, just say you remember my child, if you do.

PLEASE, just let me talk about my child.

PLEASE, just let me cry.[14]

Chapter 3

IF YOU WANT TO HELP, LISTEN

IF YOU WANT TO HELP ANOTHER PERSON, just be there. Your presence does wonders. If you want to help another person, just listen. One of the greatest gifts one person can give to another is the gift of listening. It can be an act of love and caring. But far too many people in conversations only *hear* one another. Few actually *listen*.

One person said that if we could listen to all the conversations of the world, we would discover that for the most part they are dialogues of the deaf.

Do you know what it is really like to listen to your friend—not just hear him, but really listen? Look at these verses from the Word of God that tell us how God listens to us:

> The eyes of the Lord are toward the righteous, And His ears are open to their cry. The face of the Lord is against evildoers, To cut off the memory of them from the earth. The righteous cry and the Lord hears, And delivers them out of all their troubles. The Lord is near to the brokenhearted, And saves those who are crushed in spirit. (Psalm 34:15–18 NASB)

> I love the Lord, because He hears My voice and my supplications. Because He has inclined His ear to me, Therefore I shall call upon Him as long as I live. (Psalm 116: 1–2 NASB)

Anyone who answers without listening is foolish and confused. (Proverbs 18:13 NCV)

Any story sounds true until someone tells the other side and sets the record straight. (Proverbs 18:17 TLB)

The wise man learns by listening; the simpleton can learn only by seeing scorners punished. (Proverbs 21:11 TLB)

Let every man be quick to hear [a ready listener]. (James 1:19 AMP)

Helping others means our ears and our eyes are open. What do we mean by listening? What do we mean by hearing? Is there a difference? Definitely. Hearing involves gaining content or information for your own purposes. This *isn't* helping. Listening involves caring for and being empathetic toward the friend who is talking. Hearing means that you are concerned about what's going on inside *you* during the conversation. We've all done this. Listening means that you're trying to understand the feelings of *the other person* and are listening for his or her sake. This *is* helping.

What Is Listening Really All About?

Listening means you're not thinking about what you're going to say when the other person stops talking. You are not busy formulating your response. You're concentrating on what is being said. If a hurting person intrudes upon your time and space you're likely to do this. Can you stop what you're doing to give the person your full attention?

Listening means that you're completely accepting of what is being said, without judging what your friend is saying or how he is saying it. If you don't like his tone of voice or you can't condone what he's doing and you react on the spot, you may miss the meaning. Perhaps it hasn't been said in the best way, but listen and be accepting of your friend when he is hurting. Acceptance doesn't mean that you agree with the content of what he says; it means you acknowledge and understand that what he's saying is something he is feeling. This goes such a long way in helping others.

Listening means being able to repeat what your friend said and express what you think he is feeling while speaking to you. Real listening implies having a sincere interest in the other's feelings and opinions and attempting to understand those feelings from his perspective.

Listening to another means letting go of your concerns, wants, and investments in your own position long enough to consider that friend. When you are doing the talking, you're not usually learning. But you learn when you listen. And when you listen it's hard for you to talk.

Listening is a learnable skill. Your mind and ears can be taught to hear more keenly; your eyes can be taught to see more clearly. You can also learn to *hear* with your eyes and *see* with your ears. Jesus said: "Therefore I speak to them in parables; because while seeing they do not see, and while hearing they do not hear, nor do they understand" (Matthew 13:13 NASB).

The word *hear* in the New Testament does not usually refer to an auditory experience. It usually means to pay heed. As you listen to another, you need to pay attention to what he or she is saying as well as not saying or cannot say. It requires tuning in to the right frequency.

Because of my retarded son, Matthew, who didn't have a vocabulary, I learned to listen with my eyes. I learned to read the message in his nonverbal signals. This translated to my listening to what my counselees could not put into words. I learned to listen to the message behind the message—the hurt, the ache, the frustration, the loss of hope, the fear of rejection, the feeling of betrayal, the joy, the delight, the promise of change.

I also learned to reflect upon what I saw on another's face and in his posture, walk, and pace. Then I shared with him what I saw. This provided him an opportunity to explain further what he was thinking and feeling. He knew I was tuned in to him. Your friend needs to sense that you're in sync with him. Listen with your eyes to what he or she can't put into words.

Every message your friend shares has three parts: (1) the actual content, (2) the tone of voice, and (3) the nonverbal communication. It's possible to use the same word, statement, or question and express many different messages simply by changing tone of voice or body movement. Nonverbal communication includes facial expression, body posture, and gestures or actions.

It's been suggested that successful communication consists of 7 percent content, 38 percent tone of voice, and 55 percent nonverbal communication. We're usually aware of the content of what we're saying, but not nearly as aware of our tone of voice. We have the capability of giving one sentence a dozen different meanings just by changing our tone. Tape-record some of your conversations and then listen to yourself. You'll be amazed.

When you say with the proper tone of voice, "I want to hear what you have to say," but then bury your head in paper work or check your watch, what is your friend to believe? When you ask, "How was your day?" in a flat tone while walking by him, what does he respond to—the verbal or nonverbal message?

Sometimes we wonder why our friend responds in a different way than we expected. It could have been our tone or nonverbals or the fact that he was emotionally upset.

Types of Listening

Some people listen for facts, information, and details for their own use. Others listen because they feel sorry for the person. Your friend doesn't need this. On occasion, people listen out of obligation, out of necessity, or to be polite. If you do, your friend will pick this up. Some who listen are nothing more than voyeurs who have an incessant need to pry and probe into other people's lives.

Some listen because they care. Sensitive listening and hearing are open mine shafts to really ministering to another. But all too often the potential for listening lies untapped within us like unmined gold because of barriers that inhibit our listening.

Why do you listen? What are your motives? The above reasons? Listening that springs from caring builds closeness, reflects love, and is an act of grace. And this is what Jesus calls us to do.

When you paraphrase what your friend is saying, he will continue to talk. And when you verbally agree with him, he will likely share even more. Remember this: In helping another, you need to create an environment so the hurting person feels it's safe to say what he's struggling with. If you're talking more than 25 percent of the time, it's probably too much.

Reasons We Listen

Why do we listen to others? Partly because we've been taught to do so. But there are four basic reasons why we listen to other people:

1. To understand someone—a hurting person needs this.

2. To enjoy the other person—you may not enjoy him at this time.

3. To learn something from the one talking—you will, and it may shock you!

4. To give help, assistance, or comfort to the person—this is a major reason.

The world is made up of many pseudolisteners who masquerade as the real product. But anyone who has not listened for the above reasons does not *really* listen.

For caring listening to occur, we need to be aware of some of the common obstacles that could interrupt your helping someone.

Defensiveness

You miss the message if your mind is busy thinking up a rebuttal, excuse, or exception to what your friend is saying.

There is a variety of defensive responses. Perhaps we *reach a premature conclusion.* "All right, I know just what you're going to say." Some who are in a crisis give you one sentence, become silent for a minute, then another sentence, then more silence. It could take him several minutes to complete a thought. Wait. Honor the pauses. It could be because of his state of mind. Or he could be an introvert in personality. Introverts need time to think before they speak, and they typically take about seven seconds before they answer a question.

Two other defensive indicators may be *rehearsing our responses* and *responding to explosive words.*

Rehearsing a response (as well as other defensive postures) is not what the Scriptures call us to do as listeners. Remember this verse, "Anyone who answers without listening is foolish and confused" (Proverbs 18:13 NCV).

Explosive words create an inner explosion of emotions. Not only do we react to explosive words, but we also may consciously choose to use some words that make it difficult for the other to hear. A hurting person is highly sensitive. Just expect to hear thoughts, words, or phrases that you don't like, don't accept, or don't agree with when you're reaching out to a hurting person. If you have difficulty hearing anger, resentment, or bitterness, watch out!

Not all defensiveness is overtly expressed. Outwardly we could be agreeing, but inside we're saying just the opposite. And the hurting person could be doing this to you. Give him the opportunity to disagree. You're not there to convince him of something you believe.

Personal Biases

You may have a biased attitude toward a person who speaks in a certain tone of voice, a person of a certain ethnic group, someone of the opposite sex, someone who reminds you of a person from your past, and so on. It's true. We all struggle with this to some degree. And this could cause us to reject a person or a personality without listening to what the person has to say. In effect, we're saying, "If you are _____ (and I don't like people who are _____), I don't need to listen to you." This *will* happen to you. Just expect it. Your body language will give you away. It may be an acquaintance who comes for help. Or you may be seeing a side of your friend you've never seen before and it's shocking.

Our personal biases will affect how well we listen. It may be easier for you to listen to an angry person than to a sarcastic person; some tones or phrases may be enjoyable to listen to, others may be annoying; the repetitive phrases a person uses (and may be unaware of) could bother you (and expect repetition when anyone is upset or devastated); excessive gestures, such as talking with the hands or waving the arms, can be overly distracting.

Some are distracted from listening because of gender. They're influenced by their expectations of what is appropriate for a man to share or not share or for a woman to share or not share. What about you? Has this ever happened? The stereotypes we assign to people influence how we listen to them. We'd like to believe we're free from these. But sometimes I wonder.

Different Listening Styles

One person hears with optimism and another with pessimism. I hear the bad news and you hear the good news. If your friend shares a frustrating and difficult situation, you may stop listening because you see it as petty or insignificant. Or you may listen more closely because you view it as an act of trust in you. On which side of the coin do you live? Optimistic or pessimistic?

Lack of understanding gender differences in listening and conversation creates problems. Women will use more verbal responses to encourage the talker. They're more likely than men to use listening signals like "mm-hmm" and "yeah" just to indicate they are listening.

A man will use this response only when he's agreeing with what a woman is saying. You can see what the outcome could be! A man interprets a woman's listening responses as signs that she agrees with him. But later on, he discovers she wasn't agreeing with him at all. He didn't realize she was simply indicating her interest in what he was saying and in keeping the interchange going. A woman, on the other hand, may feel ignored and disappointed because a man doesn't make the same listening response she does. She interprets his quietness as not listening.

A man is more likely than a woman to make comments throughout the conversation, but a woman may feel bothered after she's been interrupted or hasn't been given any listening feedback. This is why many women complain, "Men always interrupt" or "They never listen to women."

Inner Struggles

We have difficulty listening when our emotional involvement reaches the point where we are unable to separate ourselves from the other person. This can be a struggle for anyone attempting to help another person. You empathize too much and take his burdens on yourself.

What a friend says may cause threatening feelings to surface, or it may activate your own past hurts. Our listening can be hindered. Can you think of a time when you listened to another person and felt so overwhelmed with feelings that you were unable to hear what the person was saying? What did you do? How were you able to keep helping your friend?

We may experience difficulty in listening if the person has certain expectations of us. If someone speaks too loudly or too softly, we may struggle to keep listening. All of these can happen when you reach out to help others or when they reach out to you for help.

The Habit of Interrupting

When we feel like the other person isn't getting to the point fast enough, we may start asking for information that would be forthcoming anyway. Have you ever found yourself saying, "Hold it. I've got a dozen ideas cooking because of what you said. Let me tell you some of them"? It's easy for our minds to wander, for we think at five times the rate we speak. If a person speaks at one hundred words a minute and you're listening at the rate of five hundred per minute, what do you do? Even though you process information faster than it can be verbalized, you can choose either to stay in pace with the speaker or let your mind wander. If you're extroverted in your personality you'll struggle with listening. Extroverts have to work at this and tend to interrupt or jump in when there's silence.

Mental Overload

The other person is loading you with too much information and you just can't handle it. You feel bombarded with all the details and don't have enough time to digest them. Your mind feels like a juggler with too many items to juggle, thus it becomes difficult to listen to anything. Relax and catch the basic theme of what's going on.

Bad Timing

Have you made comments such as: "Talk? Now? Well, this isn't the best time." "Just a minute, I need to finish this." "I'd like to listen, but I'm already late for an appointment." Choosing the right time to speak can be crucial to the listening process. However, a hurting person will probably come to you at a bad time. You need to decide if you can adapt to listen right then or set up a later time.

Physical Exhaustion

Both mental and physical fatigue makes it difficult to listen. There are times when you need to let your friend know that right now isn't a good time. But be sure to let him know that you do want to hear what he has to say.

Selective Attention

Another name for this obstacle is filtered listening—screening the information being shared. If you tend to have a negative attitude, you may ignore, distort, or reject positive messages. Often we hear what we want to hear or what fits with our mindset. If we engage in selective listening, we probably engage in selective retention. That means we remember only certain comments and situations.

Do you know what hinders you from listening?

LISTEN WITH YOUR WHOLE BODY

Concentrate on the person and the message. Give your undivided attention. Turn off the TV when your friend calls to talk. Set aside what you're doing and listen. When you listen with your heart you're helping. A pastor friend told me of being called to the home of a man who had just lost his wife. When he came into the house the man wept and hugged him. Then the pastor went and sat on the couch next to the man. He decided to wait and allow the husband to take the lead in saying something. So he waited for an hour and listened to the sounds of silence. He waited for a second hour to the sounds of silence. The man sighed. My friend broke the silence and said, "Are you hungry? Would you like me to get us a pizza?"

He said, "Oh yes, that would be great." So the pastor did. He brought it back and they ate. They each said a few words. My friend prayed briefly, patted him on the shoulder, and left. Several weeks later he was surprised to hear that this man had told a number of people he had been helped by the pastor coming over and just spending time with him. Could you have done that? It may be all that your friend needs. Just be present.

Harold Kushner described your ministry:

At some of the darkest moments of my life,
some people I thought of as friends deserted me—some
because they cared about me and it
hurt them to see me in pain; others because
I reminded them of their own vulnerability,

and that was more than they could handle.
But real friends overcame their discomfort and
came to sit with me. If they had no words to make me
feel better, they sat in silence (much better than saying,
"You'll get over it," or "It's not so bad;
others have it worse"), and I loved them for it.
   —*Living a Life That Matters*[1]

Remember:

Something happens when we listen
not just with our ears
but with our eyes.
Something happens when we wait out
a griever's words.
Something happens when we express our care
in calming ways.
Something happens
when we keep our promises
even when less than convenient.
Something happens when we pay attention
to the questions of the griever
rather than offer a cheap answer.
Something happens when hearts touch.
Something happens when we remember
Jesus' promise
"Where two or three are gathered . . .
there I will be, too."
Something happens when a caregiver
Becomes a grief sharer.
   —Smith[2]

Chapter 4

Understanding What Your Friend Is Experiencing

LIFE IS FULL OF LOSSES. In fact, life is a blending of loss and gain, loss and acquisition.

Any event that destroys our understanding of the meaning of life is felt as a loss. Our beliefs and expectations come under attack.

Losses can be obvious—a stolen car, a burglarized house, or losing a loved one through death or divorce. Other losses may not be so obvious. Changing jobs, receiving a B instead of an A in a college course, receiving a less-than-hoped-for amount in a raise, moving, illness (loss of health), a new teacher in midsemester, the change from an office with windows to one without, success or achievement (the loss of striving or challenge or even relationships with fellow workers); or a son or daughter going off to school. The loss of an ideal, a dream, or a lifelong goal—all these are losses. But because these losses may not be easy to recognize, we do not identify them as losses. As one person said, "There's no casserole parade for these losses." Therefore, most don't spend time and energy dealing with them.

Many of the losses in life are related to aging. As we grow older the dreams and beliefs of childhood begin to crumble and change.

The job market contains many losses. Someone else gets the raise or promotion, deals fall through, court cases are lost, businesses fail, the economy falters, we get stuck in a "going nowhere" job.

Then we see the physical losses—a major one involves the gain of pounds and inches! We lose our youth, beauty, smooth skin, muscle tone, shape, hair, vision, hearing, and sexual ability or interest.

The loss of children (when they move out and establish their own families) can be complicated. For some it involves the loss of identity as a parent, the loss of influence over the children, the loss of dreams or feelings of success if the children didn't turn out well, and the loss of marriage if the children were the glue.

Losing a spouse when someone is older is limiting as well, but for women it is even more difficult. Most women who are over fifty and lose their husband do not remarry. If a person divorces or a spouse dies when someone is young, it is much easier to find another mate.[1]

When the word *loss* is mentioned, death and divorce come to mind. But what about the impact of a diagnosis? "The doctor said it was cancer" or multiple sclerosis or Parkinson's. Or a disability. Where is the ritual in our culture to commemorate the grief of a life-long disability? This is a state of chronic grief.

The hardest losses of life are the threatened losses. The possibility of them occurring is very present. But there is little that someone can do about them. Our sense of control is destroyed. You've worked for nineteen years at the same company. At twenty years all your benefits will be secure. But then you are informed that due to the sluggish economy and lost contracts, 40 percent of the firm's employees will be terminated at the end of the month, and length of employment is no criteria for being retained. Will you be one of the 40 percent?

There are many other threatened losses in life:

- awaiting the outcome of a biopsy
- a spouse saying, "I'm thinking of divorcing you."
- a business investment that may not come through

- being sued by an angry employee or customer
- being in a foreign country and the government threatens to detain everyone as hostages
- a friend telling us he suspects our son has been using drugs

All of the above are potential losses. They could occur. There is little we can do about them, and we feel the loss before it occurs. . . . We feel helpless.

TYPES OF LOSSES

The losses we experience in life can be grouped or identified in numerous ways. Several major types of loss could impact any of your friends.

One is the area of *material loss*. This could be the loss of a physical object or even familiar surroundings to which a person has an important attachment.

A *relationship loss* is the ending of opportunities to relate to another person. It involves talking with him, sharing experiences, touching, negotiating, conflicting, and being in the emotional and physical presence of another human being. This loss can come from a move, a divorce, a death, or just growing up.

There are also *intrapsychic losses* in which our perception or the way we view ourselves undergoes a change. We lose an emotionally important image of ourselves as well as the possibilities of what might have been.

We're all aware of a *functional loss* such as muscular or neurological function of our body. This comes with aging but also all through our life. *Memory losses* among the elderly can be devastating.

Role loss impacts all of us. It's a loss of a social role or an accustomed place in some social network. The significance of it is how much of our identity was tied in to this role. A promotion, demotion, loss of a spouse, change of career, no longer being a student, or retirement all fit here.

During the experience of loss, questions fester beneath the surface but at some point need to be addressed by your friend. You may hear these verbalized:

"Will I recover from this loss? Will I survive?"

"Is it all right to continue with my life without whatever (or whoever) has been lost to me?"

"Can I be happy and fulfilled knowing that the person I've lost is really gone and my life will now be different?"

ADJUSTING TO THE LOSS OF A FAMILY MEMBER

The loss of significant people in our lives is inevitable. Often the loss happens suddenly and traumatically. At other times the loss is expected. Either way, it can be a tremendous crisis and can sometimes bring a significant loss of identity for your friend. (If you know the person whom your friend lost you'll be feeling a loss as well. But to help your friend, some of the intensity of your grief may have to be put on hold for a while as you assist.)

For example, since 1988 I've lost three cousins, two uncles, a sister-in-law, my mother, my mother-in-law, and my son. When the loss is a highly significant person, we feel pain, and nothing and no one can prepare us for the extent of that pain. Has anyone told your friend, or you for that matter, what to expect when there's a loss of parents, a sibling, a child, or a friend? I doubt it. But most of us will experience such a loss. We grieve when a major loss like this occurs. We call it "grief work" because grieving is work.

When your friend loses a significant person, he will not only grieve over the person he lost, but also over the wishes, the needs, hopes, dreams, and unfulfilled expectations he had for the person. And these are important issues you need to help your friend identify. He may also grieve not just for his present loss, but for what he will lose in the future. Perhaps there was something he never had in his relationship with that person, and now he realizes he'll never have it. Over the years I've worked with numerous women who didn't have good relationships with their father. And when he died, that shut the door on any hope they had for reconciliation.

When your friend loses a significant person in a sudden, unexpected death, he's at high risk for a pattern of complicated grieving. This includes those who lost loved ones in the attacks on September 11, 2001, as well as the survivors. Sometimes the grief response evolves to a condition known as Post Traumatic Stress Disorder (PTSD). Why does this happen? Consider the cumulative effect of the following factors when anyone's capacity to cope crumbles:

- Your assumption about control, predictability, and security are lost.
- Your loss makes no sense whatever.
- It's difficult to recognize the loss.
- You can't even say good-bye or conclude any unfinished business.
- Your emotional reactions are heightened much more than when a natural death occurs.
- Your symptoms of grief and shock persist, which demoralizes you.
- You may tend to hold yourself responsible more than you normally would.
- You experience a profound loss of security and confidence in your world. In fact, you're shattered.
- You tend to focus on the negative aspects of the relationship with the deceased, rather than having a balanced view.
- You have sudden major secondary losses because of the unexpectedness of the loss.

All of these factors could lead anyone to experience PTSD.[2]
You may be thinking, *I could* never *help a friend in this situation.*

But you can. The more you know about this the more you will ease your fear and concern. And in many cases a friend will be the only support a person has. So the more you know, the better helper you'll be. As your friend recovers from a significant crisis or loss, at times he may be ambushed by grief (and it could hit you as well). There's no other way to describe it. Some call it a "grief spasm." It's an ongoing onslaught of grief that hits a person suddenly when he least expects it. He may choke up or cry, his chest may feel constricted and a wave of sadness may overwhelm him. This is a normal response, but when it happens he needs to stop everything else and deal with his feelings.[3]

The purpose of facing this is to come to the place where your friend can accept and live with the loss of a significant person in a healthy way. You'll be asked, "How long will this take?" You can't give him a precise answer since there are many factors to consider. But you can describe general patterns to expect.

One of the tasks of grief is to learn how to function without the other person in his life. Your friend won't have the interactions and validation he was used to experiencing with that person. Talking about this can be helpful. The loss of the physical presence in his life means that his needs, hopes, dreams, expectations, feelings, and thoughts will change. Slowly, over time, the reality of separation will begin to sink in and he will realize, "For now, I exist without this person as a part of my life." This is an important place to arrive.

Your friend may discover that it will take time to identify all the ways this individual was a part of his life. It's a step-by-step process. The loss of his companionship, support, judgment—all of these are new and separate losses that make up the major loss of his life.

Each time he starts to respond to the person who is no longer there, he'll discover again that he or she is gone. There will be many painful reminders. Your friend may say to you, "I turned to him to take care of a task he usually handled for me. Then I realized that he was gone."

Whenever someone is gone from anyone's life, roles and skills have to broaden to function without the person. Your friend will need to learn to make up for what he has lost. He changes what he does, takes over new responsibilities, and finds other people to help. There may be some things he doesn't do anymore. Adjustment necessitates not behaving the same way he did when the person was a part of his world. (This is also true when anyone loses a significant activity in his life through job loss, expulsion from school, loss of a house, and so on.)

Steps in the Grief Work Process

Getting on with life involves several steps, some of which may come as a surprise to your friend and you if you've not been through this before. Few people are aware of these steps before they experience a major loss.

Some individuals either resist these steps or become stuck in their grief work. Your presence can help to keep this from happening. Sometimes after people have gone through these stages they are able to sit down and identify what they have experienced. But what a difference it can make in their life if they're aware of the process at the time they're going through it. The awareness doesn't necessarily lessen the pain, but it gives them a map and lets them know they're on track and not going crazy. These steps apply to the more serious kinds of losses.

One of the first things your friend must do is *develop a new relationship* with the person he lost. He has to untie the ties that connected him to this person. The change involves keeping the loved one alive in his memory in a healthy and appropriate manner. Are you comfortable in talking with him about this? Is this something you've been through? If he doesn't think about it, you may need to suggest it. (You may want to suggest some resources including *Recovering From the Losses of Life*, by H. Norman Wright, Baker Books, and *Will*

My Life Ever Be the Same? by H. Norman Wright, Harvest House. If his loss was a spouse, suggest *Getting to the Other Side of Grief,* by Susan J. Zonnebelt-Smeenge and Robert C. De Vries, Baker Books.)

Formation of a new identity without the other person's presence in his life is another step to take in recovery. As one person said, "That portion of my life is history. I'll never be that way or be that person again."

THE LOSS OF A SPOUSE

Most couples who marry dream of growing old together. But when a death occurs, there is not only the loss of that dream but all sorts of secondary losses as well. Hopes, wishes, fantasies, feelings, expectations, and the needs that he had for his spouse are gone.

There's another loss in their future as well with the death of a spouse. One's identity is now being a widow or widower, a single person rather than a married one. That's a big adjustment. When a husband loses a wife, he loses someone with whom he would have shared retirement, birthdays, the bed, church functions, children and grandchildren, and weddings. Look at all the roles a spouse fulfills and what is lost when he or she dies:

friend	parent
handyperson	protector
lover	organizer
gardener	provider
companion	cook
sports partner	bill payer
checkbook balancer	laundry person
mechanic	confidant
encourager	mentor
motivator	prayer partner
business partner	source of inspiration or insight
errand person	teacher
tax preparer	counselor

As your friend walks through these steps and does his grief work, the emotional energy he once invested in his spouse is now freed up and reinvested in other people, activities, and hopes that in turn can give emotional satisfaction back to him.

Death ends a loved one's life but not your friend's relationship with that person. How does he develop a new relationship with the person he has lost? This isn't a morbid or odd process. It's a normal response. Yet, have you ever heard a discussion about such a relationship? Probably not. If people tell your friend that the best way to deal with his loss is to forget the person, very frankly, they're wrong. You don't forget. Someday, way in the future, the emotional memories will become more of historical memories.

Everyone keeps others alive all the time as we reflect upon who they were, their achievements, and their impact upon us and society. Haven't you heard people say, "I wonder what he would think if he were alive today," or, "Wouldn't she be surprised to see all of this!"? I know I have. And this is normal.

It may help your friend to be with others who have experienced the same type of loss, for they can assist him in the process of adjusting to his new identity. You may be that person.

THE LENGTH OF THE MOURNING PROCESS

How long does it take to recover and complete the mourning process? Much longer than most people believe. The amount of time can vary, depending on many factors.

The average length of mourning is approximately two years for a natural death. In the case of a terminally ill individual, the time following the death could be less, since some of the grieving happened prior to the death.

The unanticipated nature of accidental death can be a major factor in contributing to a grief reaction that lasts for several years. One study indicated that the majority of mourners who experienced the loss of a spouse or child in an automobile accident were still dealing with the death in thoughts, memories, and feelings four to seven years afterward.[4] It could take longer if your friend was involved in the same accident. And if it's a trauma there's no way to predict how long.

You can't tell your friend how long his grief will last. But be sure he'll ask you. You see, grief has a beginning, a middle, and an end. But many people get stuck in the middle, and most don't understand the dynamics and the duration of grief. This makes it even more difficult to adjust.

The emotional upheaval associated with bereavement includes a number of common elements: a sense of yearning and searching; a sensitivity to stimuli; feelings of anger, guilt, ambiguity, impatience, and restlessness; and a strong need to test what is real. As you can see from the chart on the next page, these feelings intensify and fade in peaks and valleys.

INTENSITY PHASES OF BEREAVEMENT[5]

Notice the jagged peaks. The pain and grief actually intensify at three months and then gradually subside, but not steadily. They go up and down. Most people experience a rush of grief and pain at the first-year anniversary of the loss of a loved one that rivals the initial feelings. If anyone tries to tell your friend he should be "over it by now" or "feeling better" at any of those peak times, he may become quite upset. Why he's upset is understandable. It's also understandable that people don't appreciate the grief process unless they've been through it themselves.[6]

Time after time I've shown this chart in seminars, and people have come up and said, "Why didn't someone warn me about the three-month and one-year anniversary? It would have made it easier to handle. I thought I was going crazy!" Another problem is that most feel that after three months of grieving, a person ought to be doing all right. So they pull their support away at a time when the one in grief needs it more than ever.

There's another phenomenon your friend may experience but not want to share with you or anyone else. It's called the "face in the crowd" syndrome. He's walking along and could just swear he "saw" his loved one at a gathering and heard his loved one's voice. Or he walked into a room on their anniversary and smelled her perfume. This is normal. The grieving person doesn't think it is. He'll say it's "weird," "abnormal," or "crazy." It's none of these. These experiences can last up to eighteen months after the loss.

Phases of Bereavement

THE LOSS OF A PARENT

Parental loss we all expect, but that doesn't lessen the impact. The first death I experienced with a family member came when I was twenty-two. My father was killed in a traffic accident driving home from work. He was seventy-two. What I remember was the devastating news and shock. When my mother died in 1993 at the age of ninety-three, it was a loss but not a shock. Her illness was gradual, and she had wanted to go home to be with the Lord for several years.

When Dad died, there was a sense of missing out on future events, especially since my wife and I discovered the week after the accident that we were going to be parents. Losing the first parent can often be a lingering pain as you constantly witness the effects of this loss on the remaining parent. And you can feel added pressure as you feel responsible in a new way for helping this parent.

When someone loses a parent, he loses a person who for many years has been the most influential person in his life. For most of us, losing a parent means losing someone who loved us and cared for us in a way no one else does or ever will again. We can no longer gain our parent's approval, praise, or permission. Feelings of attachment to a parent are unique.

When your friend's parent dies he loses his direct link to the past as well as to parts of himself he may have forgotten. Not only that, he will be much more aware of his own mortality. And you'll hear your friend express this. What he doesn't need to hear is, "What are you talking about? You're nowhere near your parent's age. That's ridiculous." We all feel more vulnerable because our parents aren't there to buffer life's ups and downs. When the second parent dies, it's like the last chapter of a book. For some it means they can never go home again, psychologically or physically. When you or your friend has to close up a parent's home and sort through what is left, you experience an abundance of secondary losses.

As we grow older, we often become attached to our parents in a new way. Now it's more of an adult-to-adult or friend-to-friend relationship. I saw this in the closeness of my wife and her mother. The roles reverse from the parent caring for the child to the child caring for the parent. And when Joyce's mother died, even though she was in her nineties and wanted the Lord to take her, it was painful for Joyce.

Responses to the death of a parent vary from person to person, depending on the quality of the relationship. One of your friends may grieve extensively and another move right on. If there's been a good relationship with a parent, there's the wish it could continue. There's a feeling of being let down when a parent has been taken away. For others, the loss is also the loss of opportunity to make up for difficulties in the past. Some feel cheated that they lost out on doing more for their parent(s).

And for some there may be a sense of relief. Some lived with the fear they would someday lose their parents and now it's a reality. Now they can plan to go on with their life.

For many people, the person they were closest to wasn't a birth parent. It may have been an aunt or uncle or even a surrogate parent. It's important that they face what they are feeling with this loss, experience the fullness of the grief and all the secondary losses, and then move forward without the person.

Not everyone has a good relationship with his or her parents. This can complicate the grief response. In some cases I've seen a person express relief over the death of a parent. If you heard this from a friend, how would you react? Finally your friend feels a freedom from conflict and pain. For many it's a new chance on life, an opportunity not to have to try to please someone he could never please. He may feel relief from the demands he's struggled with for years. Or he may feel relief because his parent's lingering terminal illness made it difficult to care for him or her and was financially draining. This may not have been your experience and this might shock you, especially if you hear some very negative comments.

As your friend grieves the loss of a parent, keep in mind his other family members will grieve differently because of the quality of their relationships with the parent. His siblings, spouse, and children had a different relationship than he did. This could generate conflict unless everyone allows for these differences.

When parents are gone, who takes their place or continues their role? Perhaps they were the peacekeepers for all the children and grandchildren. Who does that now? Perhaps they orchestrated the family get-togethers. Who takes on that role now? Decisions concerning home and property must be made and family heirlooms divided up. The passing of parents will definitely affect their relationship with siblings.[7]

Consideration of some of these changes in advance makes it easier for the surviving family members. These are issues and topics to address at the appropriate time. And if you don't assist your friend at this time, who will?

Chapter 5

UNDERSTANDING A FRIEND IN CRISIS

CRISIS—IT'S AN EXPERIENCE that can stop you in your tracks and immobilize you. You're thrown off balance into a state of panic and defeat. All a person wants at this time is relief! It can hit you suddenly or be the last straw in a series of small events.

People will make some of the greatest changes in their lives when they experience a crisis. They're forced to change, since the way they used to solve problems doesn't work anymore. So they're looking for solutions. Your friend may see you as the solution!

What is experienced as a crisis by your friend may not be a crisis to you. You have to see it through her eyes. And to help a friend in crisis you need to understand what constitutes a crisis.

Remember that underlying any crisis is a loss or series of losses. Your friend won't be herself; she will be different. It's as though someone came up to her and hit her over the head with a two-by-four. She's stunned. Her world isn't the same any longer. Her brain is in turmoil. The right side of the brain (the emotional side) has been overwhelmed, which results in an overwhelmed left side (the thinking side). And so in this state a friend reaches out to you.

What is your friend likely to want from you when she talks to you at a time of crisis? People's needs vary. Don't be surprised by the wide range of requests you hear. In many cases, you'll be expected to be a miracle worker. You may be her last hope, and expectations can be excessive, unrealistic, or both. When you can't produce what she wants, don't be surprised if you hear disappointment or anger. Yet you will be able to help in other ways that will meet some of her needs.

What are the different responses you may see from a friend?

You may see someone who wants a strong person to protect and control her. "Please take over for me." (You can't.)

Another may need someone who will help her maintain contact with reality. "Help me know that I am real." (This you can do.)

It could be a friend feels exceedingly empty and needs loving. "Care for me." (This you can do.)

Some need a helper to be available for a feeling of security. "Always be there." And she may call you constantly. (This won't work. Helping is a part-time endeavor, not a full-time job.)

Or you may see the following:

A person with obsessive guilt who is driven to confess. "Take away my guilt." (Only the Lord can do this.)

An urgent need to talk things out. "Let me get it off my chest." (You can listen—remember the definition.)

Demanding advice on pressing issues. "Tell me what to do." (Be careful. Help her discover the options.)

A person who seeks to sort out her conflicting ideas. "Help me to put things into perspective." (This is possible.)

Can you think of other needs? In some situation, your friend may come with *all* of these, making *you* feel overwhelmed.

CHARACTERISTICS OF THOSE IN CRISIS

Of the various friends who seek your help, some will cope quite well with their crises while others cope quite poorly. It is possible to predict which will be which. You need to be on alert for these characteristics.

Overwhelmed. The first characteristic of people who cope poorly is that they are nearly overwhelmed in a crisis. Why? Prior to the crisis they were already struggling emotionally. Now they respond in a way that makes matters worse, but from their perspective they're doing the most efficient thing possible.

Poor physical condition. The second characteristic of those who cope poorly in a crisis is a poor physical condition. They have fewer resources to draw on during a crisis.

Hard time coping. Those who deny reality have a hard time coping with a crisis. Denying reality is their attempt to avoid their pain and anger. They may deny that they're seriously ill or financially ruined or that their child is on drugs or terminally ill.

Magic of the mouth. This is the tendency to eat, drink, smoke, and talk excessively. When difficulty enters these people's lives, they seem to regress to infantile forms of behavior. Their mouths take over in one way or another. Do you have any friends like this? They're uncomfortable unless they are doing something with their mouths most the time. This attempt to not face the real problem can continue after the crisis is over. The person is actually helping to create an additional crisis for herself.

Unrealistic approach to time. People who cope this way crowd the time dimensions of a problem, or they extend the time factors way into the future. In other words, they want the problem to be "fixed" right away, or else they delay and delay. Delaying avoids the discomfort of reality but enlarges the problem. If your friend does this, be prepared for a difficult time in helping.

Excessive guilt. Those who struggle with excessive guilt will have difficulty coping with a crisis. Why? They tend to blame themselves for the difficulty, and by feeling worse immobilize themselves even more.

Blamers. Blamers have a difficult time coping with a crisis. They don't focus on what the problem is but turn to "who caused the problem." Their approach is to find some enemies, either real or imagined, and project the blame upon them.

Excessive dependence or independence. These friends either turn away from offers to help or become a clinging vine. The one who clings tends to suffocate you if you're involved in helping her. She'll call you several times a day. Boundaries have little meaning to her. An overly independent friend will shun your offer to help, and even if she is sliding down the hill toward disaster, she doesn't cry out for assistance. When the disaster hits, she either continues to deny it or blames others for it.

One other characteristic must be cited that has a bearing upon all the others. A person's theology will affect how he or she copes with a crisis. Our lives are based upon our theology, and yet so many people are frightened by that word. Our belief in God and how we perceive God is a reflection of our theology. Those who believe in the sovereignty and caring nature of God have a better basis from which to approach life.

PHASES OF A CRISIS

We will now look at the typical pattern that occurs in a person's life as he or she goes through the change and crisis sequence. As you can see from the chart, there are four phases in any life-changing event or crisis.

Impact

The impact phase is usually very brief. A person knows immediately that she has been confronted with a major happening. For some people it is like being hit with a two-by-four. The impact phase involves becoming aware of the crisis and experiencing the effect of being stunned. This period lasts from a few hours to a few days depending upon the event and the person involved. In a severe loss,

THE NORMAL CRISIS PATTERN[1]

	Phase I Impact	Phase II Withdrawal/Confusion	Phase III Adjustment	Phase IV Reconstruction/ Reconciliation
Time:	Few Hours to a Few Days	Days to Weeks	Weeks to Months	Months
Response:	Should I stay and face it or withdraw?	Intense emotions. You feel drained. Anger, sadness, fear, anxiety, depression, rage, guilt.	Your positive thoughts begin returning along with all the emotions.	Hope has returned. Self-confidence.
Thoughts:	Numb, disoriented. Insight ability limited. Feelings overwhelm.	Thinking ability limited. Uncertainty and ambiguity.	You're now able to problem solve.	Thinking is clearer.
Direction You Take to Regain Control:	You search for what you lost.	Bargaining/wishful thinking. Detachment.	You begin to look for something new to invest in.	Progress is evident and new attachments are made to something significant.
Searching Behavior:	Often reminiscing	Puzzled, unclear.	You can now stay focused and begin to learn from your experience.	You may want to stop and evaluate where you've been and where you're going.

Emotional Level

tears can occur immediately or a few days later. The more severe the crisis or loss the greater the impact and the greater the amount of incapacitation and numbness.

It is possible for the impact phase to linger on and on, as in the case of a divorce proceeding. During this phase, the person has to make a decision whether to stay and fight the problem through to resolution or run and ignore the problem. We call this the fight-or-flight pattern. During the impact stage your friend is usually less competent than normal, and her usual tendency of handling life's problems will probably emerge. If the tendency in the past has been to face problems, she will probably face the problem now. But if her tendency has been to avoid problems, she will probably run from this one.

Fighting and attempting to take charge again in the midst of crisis seem to be the healthier responses. Running away only prolongs the crisis. And as each of the succeeding phases is dependent upon the adjustments made in the previous one, avoiding reality does not make for good judgment. Pain is prolonged instead of resolved.

Lessened Thinking Capability: Thinking capability is lessened during the impact stage. People are somewhat numb and disoriented. It is even possible for some to feel as though they cannot think or feel at all. It is as though their entire system shut down. Insight is lessened and should not be expected at this time. The factual information you give your friend may not fully register at this time and may have to be repeated later on. (This is why suggestions, plans you make together, etc., need to be written down in order to be remembered.) You may explain something to her, and she in turn asks a question that indicates she never heard one word. Because she's numb and stunned, she may make unwise decisions. But, unfortunately, important decisions may be necessary; postponing them may not be an option. This is where she needs your help. And if you don't have the answers, ask for help yourself.

Searching for the Lost Object: During the impact phase, a person physically and symbolically searches for the lost object. Her thought process is directed toward the loss. It's common for your friend who loses a loved one in death to take out photographs and other items that remind her of the person who died. When something that means a great deal to us is lost, we hold on to our emotional attachments longer than we normally would. It's normal to search for the lost object or a replacement, and the searching is greater when we aren't aware of what is happening to us.

Reminiscing about the loss is in proportion to the value of the lost object or person. Your friend needs to be listened to and have her feelings accepted at this point of the crisis. Feeling rejected delays the resolution of the problem. Feelings shouldn't be buried or denied at this point. The person may even feel strange about the feelings and thoughts she's experiencing. Negative comments from others don't help at all. If you are feeling discomfort as you help a person in crisis, your friend may shut down her feelings. Instead, take time to discover the source of your own discomfort, for in doing this you will become better able to respond to life yourself and to help others.

Feelings of Guilt: The emotion of guilt frequently accompanies change and crisis. People feel guilty for many reasons, from having failed to having achieved. Many people have difficulty handling success. They wonder if they deserve it, or perhaps they see others who did not succeed and in their empathy for them experience guilt over their own success. Children of parents who divorce sometimes feel guilty as though they were responsible for the destruction of the marriage. Those who witness accidents or catastrophes often experience guilt. "Why was I spared?" "Why did my young child die and not me? He had so many more years left than I did!" are common reactions.

A friend experiencing guilt has several choices available to her to alleviate the guilt. She can rationalize her way out of the guilt. She can project blame onto others. She can attempt to pay penance and work off the guilt. Or she can apply the forgiveness available where there has been genuine sin and violation of God's principles. God can and does remove true guilt. But there will be other feelings of guilt that have no basis. A person who lives on her emotions most of the time will be more guilt-prone during a crisis than others. Those who have negative patterns of thinking or self-talk will exhibit guilt more than others. Forgiveness from God is not usually needed for false guilt. What is needed is help in changing her perspective or self-talk. But this will take time and will probably not be accomplished during the impact phase.

Before we go on to the next stage, let me explain how the use of the previous chart has been helpful for those in crisis. Often this person feels overwhelmed and wonders, "Is my response normal?" On many occasions I have shown people the complete chart, described the various stages, and asked them to indicate where they were on the chart. I usually do this during the second phase, "Withdrawal/Confusion." They respond by first identifying which stage they are in and then saying, "You mean, my response is normal?" By discovering the normalcy of their response, they feel relieved. Then they're able to see where they will be heading, which further alleviates their anxiety. I carry a laminated copy of the chart with me in my Bible. You may want to do the same.

Withdrawal/Confusion

Intensity in the Emotional Level: One of the key factors in the withdrawal/confusion phase is the intensity in the emotional level. The shock has worn off and those underlying feelings intensify. If you look back at the chart, you will note that each phase becomes progressively longer. This phase, typically the second phase, can last days and even weeks.

Denies Feelings: During this phase, the tendency to deny one's feelings is probably stronger than at any other time. Feelings now can become ugly and most potent. Intense anger can occur toward whatever happened, which in some cases brings on guilt for having such feelings. Depression, sadness, fear—these are all part of the denial. Shame can then result, and the pain of all the various feelings can bring the tendency and desire to suppress all feelings. Christians and non-Christians alike refuse to let the process of grief occur. This denial leads to emotional, physical, and interpersonal difficulties in time. The best step you can take in helping a friend is to help her identify and put words to her feelings and normalize them, using another chart, the Ball of Grief (see next page).

Make a copy of this to give to your friend. I use the chart in two ways. One way is that I ask the person to identify which of these feelings she is experiencing. Another way is to ask which of these she *isn't* experiencing. Once again you will have a friend ask, "You mean these are normal responses?" And you can respond with, "Definitely." Encourage your friend to take this out each day to identify what she is experiencing. Often I ask the person to evaluate her fear or depression or anger on a scale of 0–10 to discover whether it is increasing or decreasing. It's a helpful way to measure improvement.

How do people actually *feel* when confronted by a crisis? What goes on in their emotional spectrum when they find they are unable to adjust to life's major difficulties? You will hear the following:

- A sense of *bewilderment*: "I never felt this way before."
- A sense of *danger*: "I feel so scared—something terrible is going to happen."
- A sense of *confusion*: "I can't think clearly—my mind doesn't seem to work."
- A sense of *impasse*: "I'm stuck—nothing I do seems to help."
- A sense of *desperation*: "I've got to do something, but I don't know what to do."
- A sense of *apathy*: "Nothing can help me—what's the use of trying."

- A sense of *helplessness*: "I can't cope by myself—please help me."
- A sense of *urgency*: "I need help now."
- A sense of *discomfort*: "I feel so miserable and unhappy."

Knowing this can assist you in relating to the person. You might make statements such as: "Could it be that you just can't think clearly? Like your mind isn't working?" "Could it be that you feel stuck, like 'Nothing I do seems to help'?" "Perhaps you feel

BALL OF GRIEF[2]
A TANGLED "BALL" OF EMOTIONS

immobilized like, 'Why try? Nothing I do seems to help.' "

If your friend's shared feelings begin to shock and alarm you, she'll tend to repress them. But they are never repressed from God. He understands and accepts her emotional state. Feelings need to be expressed, which means that friends, relatives, or you, along with a social support system, need to be available. Unfortunately, the availability of other friends and relatives might not coincide with when your friend needs help. Meals, gifts, cards, time, and prayers come during the impact phase and the beginning of the withdrawal/confusion phase. But usually in a few weeks, the support system diminishes, and that is when it may be needed most. That is one step you can take—to assist in developing an ongoing support system.

Develop a Support System: Over the years I have come in contact with more and more churches that have developed an ongoing ministry for those who have experienced the loss of a loved one. The church arranges for families to minister to the bereaved person in some way each week for a period of two years such as cards, a call, or a meal invitation. This not only involves many from the congregation in ministry, but also supports the person over an extended period.

A minister who attended one of my crisis seminars shared that following a funeral or memorial service he writes the name of the family on his desk calendar every three months for the next two years to remind him to continue to reach out and minister to them over that period of time.

During the withdrawal/confusion phase, your friend *does not* need or benefit from spiritual and psychological insights. Her emotional state, whether it be anger or depression, interferes with the information. We can only hope she will be able to draw on what she has already learned, since she will find it difficult to incorporate anything new.

One of the best ways to aid your friend during this phase is to give her some help organizing her life. She needs assistance in arranging appointments, keeping the house in order, and other routine responsibilities. People need this help because they may be suffering from some paralysis of the will.

Above all, when you work with a person in phases one or two, use sustainment responses. These are basic and simple—listening, reassurance, encouragement, and reflection. These approaches will help to lower your friend's anxiety, guilt, and tension and provide emotional support. Your task is to assist in helping her restore some balance into her life.

Self-pity: Another tendency at this phase is self-pity. It's not uncommon for your friend to appear confused. This may be evident because she will begin some task or start to approach people and then retreat. She may approach new people and situations as a type of replacement for what was lost, but then retreat to reminisce. Making a decision during this phase to replace what was lost is not a good idea. The person is not ready, for whatever or whoever was lost has not yet been fully released.

Adjustment

Notice the length of time the third phase, *adjustment*, takes—longer than the others. The emotional responses during this time are hopeful. Some depression may remain or come and go, but positive attitudes have started. Things are looking up. Your friend may talk with hope about such future possibilities as enjoying a new job or a new location, rebuilding a fire-destroyed home, or considering a remarriage. She has just about completed her detachment from what was lost and is now looking for something new to which she can become attached.

Climbing Out: What is occurring in her world begins to take on new importance to her. She has been through the depths of the valley and is now climbing out. What she begins to attach to holds special significance for her. An outsider may not see the same significance and may feel that she is making a mistake by choosing this new job, new home, or new partner. Your friend doesn't need you as a critic, for she is responding from a perspective different from yours. You need to see life through her eyes and not your own.

The one area in which we do need to caution the person is selecting a new partner. At this phase it is usually too soon, whether the loss of the spouse is through death or divorce. I encourage those who are going through a divorce to wait at least a year following the divorce to begin dating. And it's imperative that they complete a divorce recovery program as well. Recovery needs to occur first or they select a new partner from a position of weakness and the baggage they bring from their previous relationship interferes with this new one.

This may be the time to recommend books or other resources to help your friend recover. Timing is essential and you don't want to force this issue. (Several resources are mentioned at the conclusion of this chapter.)

Hopeful: Remember that your friend at this time is hopeful, but it is not a consistent sense of hope. She fluctuates and will have down times. She still needs someone to be close or available. Because insight is returning, she can be objective about what has occurred and now can process new information and suggestions. She can gain new insights spiritually at this point, and her values, goals, and beliefs may be different and have a greater depth.[3] Now is the time to ask questions like, "Where has God been in all of this for you?" "How has this impacted you spiritually?" "What have you learned through all of this that will help you the next time you hit a crisis?" "How are you a different person?"

Reconstruction and Reconciliation

A Spontaneous Expression of Hope: This is shown in a sense of confidence, and plans are made out of this sense of confidence. Doubts and self-pity are gone because your friend has made a logical decision at this point not to engage in them anymore. She takes the initiative for progress, and reattachments are occurring. New people, new places, new activities, new jobs, and new spiritual responses and depths now exist. If there has been anger and blame toward others or if relationships were broken, this is now the time for reconciliation. Helpful gestures, notes, or meals shared together and doing a helpful act for others may be the forms of reconciliation.

Reflection of Newness: The final resolution of a crisis is a reflection of the newness of a person. A crisis is an opportunity for your friend to gain new strengths, new perspectives on life, new appreciations, new values, and a new way to approach life. I have experienced the four phases of a crisis in my life. Sometimes it is possible to work one's way through the four phases in less time than indicated. And sometimes one or two of the phases may take less time because of the experienced or threatened loss.

A number of years ago I experienced some strange physical symptoms. These included vertigo, pressure in the back of the head, and headaches. These symptoms persisted for about seven weeks, during which time the doctors had some theories but nothing concrete. There was a real uncertainty, and my own concerns and worries about what this might be added to some of the feelings I experienced.

Finally, after going through further examination including a CAT scan, the symptoms disappeared. As we pieced together what had occurred, we felt the physical symptoms were brought on by too many strenuous seminars with no recuperation time in between, coupled with a cold and some altitude changes. Physical exhaustion was one of the greatest culprits. But this experience, especially at the age of forty-seven, caused me to think, reevaluate, and consider some changes. I did not necessarily like what I went through, but I grew because of it and felt it was necessary.

This is what happens in a crisis. At this time, encourage your friend in the growth you've seen. Continue to pray. The two of you could even talk about how your friend can use what she learned to help others.[4]

RESOURCES TO RECOMMEND

Loss of a Spouse
Getting to the Other Side of Grief, Susan J. Zonnebelt-Smeenge and Robert C. DeVries (Baker Books, 1998)

Loss of a Child
Confessions of a Grieving Christian, Zig Ziglar (Thomas Nelson, 1998)

Empty Arms: Hope and Support for Those Who Have Suffered a Miscarriage, Stillbirth, or Tubal Pregnancy, Pamela W. Vredevelt (Multnomah, 1994)

I'll Hold You in Heaven, Jack Hayford (Regal, 1986)

General Helps
A Bend in the Road, David Jeremiah (Thomas Nelson, 2000)

Do Not Lose Heart, Meditations of Encouragement and Comfort, Dave and Jan Dravecky (Zondervan, 1998)

Finding God's Peace in Perilous Times, Tammy Faxel, ed. A book written in response to 9/11 (Tyndale House Publishers, 2002)

Recovering From the Losses of Life, H. Norman Wright (Baker Books, 1991)

Will My Life Ever Be the Same, H. Norman Wright (Harvest House, 2002). This book specifically addresses recovering from a crisis or trauma.

Chapter 6

WHAT'S HAPPENING TO MY FRIEND? IT'S CALLED TRAUMA

THERE'S A NEW WORD IN OUR VOCABULARY. It's *trauma*. Oh, we've heard it before, but since September 11 it's taken on new significance. Events in the last ten years also have made trauma a reality.

First in 1993 at the World Trade Center, next in 1995 in Oklahoma City, then in 1996 during the Olympics, and finally in 2001 at the World Trade Center again. Americans have now joined much of the rest of the world in facing the reality of terrorism. No longer is this cowardly evil confined to foreign countries. We experienced a twenty-first-century "Day of Infamy"—and life in the United States has been altered forever. People will be suffering the aftermath of this horror for years.

Trauma is the response to any event that shatters our safe world. It's more than a state of crisis. Trauma leaves us feeling unsafe—our place of refuge has been invaded. People live with trauma right in their neighborhood, right on their block. It may have happened to you. And it's certainly happened to someone you know. Just turn on the news in the evening. We can't get away from it.

Some of the first examples of trauma go back to the story of Job, who lost his family, farm, and health suddenly and by violent means (Job 1:13–19). David had several close (and no doubt traumatic) encounters with death that involved animals, soldiers, King Saul, and giants (1 Samuel 17:1–52; 18:10–11, 27; 19:8). He also witnessed hand-to-hand combat and thousands of brutal murders. These events affected his personality and altered his immediate family. His daughter Tamar was raped by her half brother (2 Samuel 13: 10–15). His son Amnon was killed at the command of Absalom, another son, who later also died a violent death (2 Samuel 13:28–29; 18:9–15). The Bible also recounts other traumas. In Judges 19 we read about gang rape. Jonah was shipwrecked and swallowed by a big fish (Jonah 1–2). The experience of Christ on the cross was very traumatic to both Jesus and His disciples.

The word *trauma* comes from a Greek word that means "wound." It's a condition characterized by the phrase, "I just can't seem to get over it." This experience is not limited to those who have gone through a war. I've seen it in the father who saw his daughter fatally crushed in an accident years ago and in women who were sexually abused as children; those who have had an abortion have experienced it. I've seen it in the paramedic, the chaplain, and the nurse, and also in the survivor of a robbery, traffic accident, or rape. I heard it in the voice of my neighbor as he described being a witness to an armed robbery in a video store. Trauma touches those subjected to pressure or harassment in the workplace. I also saw it in the face of those impacted by the terrorist attack in New York City. Perhaps you've seen the same or even personally experienced it. You may think your friend has experienced a loss, but it could have been trauma and you may be the one to suggest he see a trauma specialist. But you need to understand what it is in order to help.

What's Trauma Like?

What we used to see as a safe world is no longer safe. What we used to see as a predictable world is no longer predictable. Most people overestimate the likelihood that life is going to be relatively free from major crises or traumas. Most underestimate the possibility of negative events happening to them. Perhaps that's why we're so devastated and our core beliefs shaken when they do. What beliefs do you and your friend hold about life? What will happen to those beliefs if either of you experiences a trauma? Will your beliefs be tested? Will they survive the testing? It's important to ask yourself these questions *before* trauma enters your life or anyone else's.

If someone has been feeling invulnerable and thinking *It can't happen to me*, trauma will not only wound him and shake his beliefs, it will fill his life with fear. If your friend has been traumatized, expect this. Invulnerability is an illusion. We don't have to be a victim of the bombing in Oklahoma City or New York City to suddenly feel vulnerable. Just viewing the ongoing vivid pictures on TV or the still photographs in the paper is sufficient to take us from the role of spectator to participant in the trauma. We all ended up feeling *If it can happen there, it can happen here*. What were you like during the weeks after 9/11? What about your friends?

We see it all the time on TV. Most newscasts carry several stories with trauma potential. We see snatches of the tragedy, usually with a scene of a memorial service, a few anguished words from a family member or victim, and then the scene quickly shifts to another tragedy. It may be the last we see or hear of it, and perhaps the last we think about it. But it's not over for those involved; it's just beginning. For some victims the trauma will go on for years. For others it will go on as long as they live.

Perhaps you're asking the question that most people ask: "How widespread are traumatic events in our country? How many people are exposed to traumatic events, such as natural and technological disasters, accidents, crime, abuse, or war?"

We used to say 75 percent of the general population in our country has been exposed to some event that meets the criteria for becoming a trauma. Now it's even higher. The good news is that only about 25 percent of those exposed to such events become traumatized.[1] But those who are traumatized need help as soon as possible.

One can experience a crisis and not end up traumatized. There are also people walking around today who think and feel that the state of trauma they are in is just the way life is meant to be lived. But it's not.

Even if you're not a traumatized person, someone you know may be. *What you understand about trauma could enable you to be a healing, supportive influence in that person's life.* It could be your presence, your normalizing his feelings, your referral that makes a difference for him.

Physical trauma affects a person in two ways. Obviously, some part of the body is impacted with such a powerful force that the body's natural protection, such as skin or bones, can't prevent the injury, and the body's normal, natural healing capabilities can't mend the injured without some assistance.

Perhaps not as obvious is the emotional wounding caused by trauma. Our psyche can be so assaulted that our beliefs about ourselves, our life, our will to grow, our spirit, our dignity, and our sense of security are damaged. Have you seen this happen to a friend? He ends up feeling helpless. People can experience this to some degree in a crisis and still bounce back. In trauma they have difficulty bouncing back because they feel derealization (*Is this really happening?*) and depersonalization (*I don't know what I really stand for anymore*).

TRAUMA'S EFFECT ON THE BRAIN

As the result of trauma, something happens in our brain that affects the way we process information. It affects how we interpret and store the event we experienced. In effect, it overrides our alarm system. Trauma has the power to disrupt how we process incoming information. When we can't handle the stress, we activate our survival techniques.[2]

Most of us aren't aware of what happens to our brain. There's an alarm portion of the brain that controls our behavior. When we've been traumatized, this alarm system becomes hypersensitive. It overreacts to normal stimuli. For example, it sees a large person and feels *He's going to hurt me. Oh no!*

But another part of the brain is analytical and calms down the emotional part of the brain—it analyzes things and puts things into perspective. *No, a large person isn't necessarily going to hurt me.*

In trauma it's as though the left side (the cognitive) and the right side (the emotional) are disconnected from one another. Usually our body, emotions, and thoughts are all connected. Trauma separates these from one another. We may have vivid graphic thoughts about what happened, but no emotion. Or we might experience intense emotions, but without the thoughts or actual memories. As one man said, "I feel like my brain was disrupted and one part is transmitting the AM and the other the FM. Sometimes there are holes in my memory like a slice was taken out. Other times I can't get those intrusive unwanted memories to stop. I want them evicted! I can't remember what I want to remember and I can't forget what I want erased." This struggle is familiar to those who undergo trauma.[3] I've heard people say, "It's like my mind was scrambled."

SUSCEPTIBILITY TO TRAUMA

Are some people more susceptible to being traumatized than others? If your friend is "emotionally healthy," if he came from a "healthy home," if he's a "strong Christian," is he immune to this disorder? No. Neither are you. We're all susceptible to trauma; we're all at risk. Our previous mental stability, race, gender, level of education, and previous emotional disorders or lack of emotional disorders seem to make no difference, although our ability to handle life's ordinary stresses and our personally developed coping skills can help. But trauma can overwhelm any of us.

If you or a friend becomes traumatized, it's *not* because of a defect in either of you. Your reactions are normal in response to an abnormal event. Your personality doesn't alter the outcome of experiencing trauma, but trauma *does* impact your personality. Yes, we do vary in our responses and our capacity for endurance. Some people have better coping skills than others. Those who have a strong faith in Jesus Christ and an accurate understanding of life through the Scriptures have more resources to help them cope. But for all of us there comes a point in time when our defenses are overrun.[4] (How many in your church understand trauma? Does your church staff?) Too often when we meet someone in trauma we're threatened because we want him to be better, to be normal (or "fixed"), and we don't know what to do. So we withdraw or do or say something that isn't helpful.

There's one last factor to consider. Those who are involved in natural catastrophes seem to experience shorter and less intense Post Traumatic Stress Disorder (PTSD) than those involved in man-made disasters. If a natural disaster can be seen as an act of nature or God—*that's just life*—the survivors don't lose as much trust in others as those involved in man-made disasters. Another word for man-made is *atrocity*. That's why Oklahoma City, Columbine, and New York City have impacted us so much. Also, those who experience one trauma usually recover more quickly than those who have experienced multiple traumas.[5]

What experiences qualify to create traumas in our lives? There are so many events. As you read the following paragraphs, consider the people you know (including yourself) who may have experienced such natural catastrophes as earthquakes, fires, floods, hurricanes, tornadoes, volcanic eruptions, landslides, or life-threatening windstorms. I've been in threatening windstorms and been jolted out of bed by earthquakes. As a teen, my family's lives were saved by our collie barking and alerting us to a fire in our home. Thankfully, none of these events were severe enough to traumatize me.

Sometimes there are community or work-related disasters such as a chemical spill or explosion.

Trauma can occur in the survivors of a refugee or concentration camp.

Many people have become traumatized through sexual or physical assault. By age eighteen, 25 percent of girls and 16 percent of boys have been sexually abused. For some children, trauma is not Oklahoma City. It's going home at night.

Children who were physically mistreated by excessive beatings, spankings, confinement, or deprivation of food or medical care can be seriously affected for life.

We can be traumatized by witnessing a death or serious injury in a car accident; by seeing a victim of a violent crime beaten, raped, or killed; by being exposed to an uprising, riot, or war.

Children, who have even less capability than adults to handle significant events in their lives, can be more easily damaged. At risk is any child who has witnessed the murder, suicide, rape, or beating of a family member, significant adult, or friend. And the number of traumatized children who experience the aftermath of gang violence in our society is growing.

Many of the conditions mentioned so far pertain to being a witness. When it happens to you, it's even worse. The list of events is extensive.

Being a combatant, prisoner, or medic in war creates the potential for trauma. Anyone who has been robbed, mugged, abducted, raped, kidnapped, terrorized, or injured in a vehicular accident experiences trauma. Any situation in which you feel that you or another family member could be killed or hurt gives you cause to experience trauma.

Those involved in the helping profession are open to trauma if they've been involved in just one of the following conditions:

- witnessed death and injury
- experienced a threat to their own safety and life
- made life-and-death decisions
- worked in high-stress conditions

This last condition includes situations like working long hours or being in an unsafe environment.

Paramedics, rescue teams (the rescue workers in the burned-out hulk of the Federal Building in Oklahoma or the divers searching for bodies underwater amidst the torn fuselage of TWA Flight 800, and all the various personnel at Ground Zero in New York City, for example), police officers, fire fighters, and medical personnel—all are at risk.

My son-in-law, who is a fire fighter, has experienced first- and second-degree burns fighting fires. He has witnessed numerous deaths and made many significant life-and-death decisions. Fire fighters frequently have to operate on very little sleep and sometimes work forty-eight-hour shifts.

Overwhelming? Very possible. But this is what happens in life.

If someone you know has experienced any of the above events, then you or that person has experienced trauma. This doesn't mean that PTSD or being traumatized is necessarily a result, but the event has potential to lead to it.[6]

And keep in mind that sometimes what is traumatic to one person may not be to another. You may be thinking, "I hope I don't have to try and help someone who's been traumatized." It will probably happen. We can't always choose who comes to us for help. We can choose to be there, to be present, to listen, and to pray. For many, this will do wonders.

Chapter 7

WHAT DOES TRAUMA DO?

TRAUMA HAS MANY EFFECTS. It shatters our beliefs and assumptions about life, challenges our belief that we have the ability to handle life, and tears apart our belief that the world is a just and orderly place to live. That's quite dramatic, isn't it? Whether it's your friend or you, here is what to expect:

Trauma leads to silence: *I don't have the words to describe it.*

Trauma leads to isolation: *No one seems to understand or enters into the experience I had.*

Trauma leads to feelings of hopelessness: *There was no way to stop what happened or the memories of what happened.*[1]

Our level of optimism begins to crumble.

We all want a reason for what happens to us. We want to know *why* so that we can once again have a sense of order and predictability about life. But in trauma we end up with unanswered questions. And your friend will have a number of them.

She might say, "I always thought right would prevail as well as justice. What happened seems so unfair!" What do we do when we expect the good guys to always win and the bad guys to always lose, and it doesn't turn out that way?

Job said it well: "Behold, I cry out of wrong, but I am not heard. I cry aloud, but there is no judgment" (Job 19:7 KJV).

We all want answers, expect answers, plead for answers, but sometimes heaven remains silent. That's when our faith undergoes a crisis in addition to whatever else is impacting us.

Trauma also affects how your friend sees herself; it affects her self-identity. We all have a picture of ourselves. She may see herself as a rational, strong, take-charge, in-control person. A trauma changes all that.

REEXPERIENCING TRAUMA

Your friend may *reexperience the trauma*. Thoughts, pictures, dreams, nightmares, or even flashbacks of what happened may occur. Sometimes it may slip into her mind like a video stuck on continuous replay. This sensitivity can become so extreme that an event can trigger a flashback and make her feel and act as if she were experiencing the original trauma all over again. This is a normal response.

One fire fighter from New York City said, "After the Trade Tower disaster I heard about others who died and it was like a carousel of faces running in front of me. There were classic pictures that will be in my head forever. I knew thirty guys who aren't here anymore. I can see them, feel them, taste them. I don't know what to make of it! There's just no language to describe what you see and feel. It's like a nightmare you can't wake up from. I see a lot of destruction but this was magnified a million times. I'm just trying to grab on to life."

A friend of mine who is a Vietnam vet often experiences a flashback at police funerals as he sees the flag-draped coffin. I've been with people who can't watch certain movies because of the effect they have on them. I've been with a person who, when the loud rumbling of a truck went by, reacted as though it was a major earthquake hitting again, similar to the one that traumatized him.

A combat veteran walks down a street and hears a car backfire. He dives behind a car to hide from the enemy and recalls the memories of his friends who were blown up in front of him. A victim of rape or sexual abuse has a flashback when making love to his or her spouse. An accident victim has a flashback at the sight of a car wreck or blood. Someone sees an object falling from a building and once again he sees people jumping from the World Trade Center.

Reminders, or triggers, can include the anniversary of the event. As the date draws near, the intensity of the actual trauma can build. Holidays and other family events can create strong emotional responses as well. It's possible for a traumatized person to be set off by something she sees, hears, smells, or tastes. In the case of abuse, a confrontation with the abuser may bring back emotional or physical reactions associated with the abuse. It helps to forewarn your friend about such a possibility.

Even the system that is designed to help a victim can cause her to relive the painful event. It could be the court system or sentencing process, the police, or the mental health system. You may need to accompany a friend to one of these encounters. Certainly the media doesn't help in their graphic coverage of the worst incidents in life, nor do the movies in their extensive portrayals of violence. These portrayals can also bring back the memories of a traumatized person's victimization.[2] Encourage your friend to avoid certain programs, especially avoiding the news at bedtime.

In a flashback it's as though the person leaves the present and travels back in time to the original event. It seems so real. She sees it, hears it, and smells it. Sometimes a person begins to react as if she were there. Your friend may be hesitant to admit this to you for fear of your reaction. A flashback is like a cry of something that needs to come out and does so in the only way it knows how. When survivors can talk about the trauma, write about it, and bring it to God in an honest and real way through worship, there isn't as great a need for this memory to be so intrusive in nightmares, images, or flashbacks. And at first your job may be that you need to not only accompany your friend to the worship service but also let others know what to expect and how to respond.

Sometimes a person reexperiences trauma not through memories or images but through *painful and angry feelings* that seem to come out of nowhere. These feelings occur because they were repressed at an earlier time. Now the emotions are simply crying out for release. Listen to them and don't take them personally.

Another way your friend may reexperience trauma is through *numbing and avoidance*. It's painful to reexperience trauma. For some, it's agonizing. She wants it to go away and disappear forever, but it doesn't. And so her body and her mind take over to protect against the pain. This is done by emotional numbing. Her defense system kicks into gear to help her adjust. When numbing occurs it can create a diminished interest in all areas of life. She may feel detached from others around her, even the ones she loves the most. Often there is no emotional expression because she's shut everything down. Your friend may tend to reduce her involvement with life.[3]

When your friend reexperiences trauma, sometimes she feels some of the emotion she didn't experience at the time of the event because of the numbing that took place. Now when feelings of rage, anger, guilt, anxiety, fear, or sadness emerge she'll wonder, "Where did these come from? They hurt! I don't want them!" She will shut down again so she won't feel as if she's going through a series of out-of-control mood swings. And then she may begin to avoid situations she thinks may trigger this condition. She might retreat from other people, from family, and even from life. She could do this mentally, socially, physically, and often spiritually. Continue to reach out but not in an offensive manner. Can you sit quietly with a person for a half an hour not saying a word? You may need to.

Your friend may stay away from the type of place where the problem occurred. If she was robbed in a restaurant, she may avoid restaurants. I've seen fire fighters, police officers, and medical personnel seek another line of work after they've been traumatized.

Those who have experienced trauma have their own set of triggers that can activate the memories of what they experienced. Listen and be alert and you may discover some of the triggers that your friend may not see at this time.

There's something else you can expect to see in a traumatized friend. She's on alert and this is usually referred to as *hyperalertness* or *hyperarousal*. The strong emotions we experience—fear, anxiety, anger—affect the traumatized person's body, particularly her adrenaline output.

During a traumatic event, the heart begins to race, breathing is difficult, and muscles tighten. Some, in an attempt to make sense of what is happening to them, mislabel their bodily responses. They may say, "I'm going crazy," "I'm going to collapse," "I'm going to have a heart attack," or "I'm dying." Some never correct the way they label these bodily responses. So anytime their heart pounds or it's hard to breathe, they misinterpret what's happening and end up with a panic attack.[4] This could be frightening to you if you've never seen a panic attack.

For some victims of trauma, emotions—such as fear—rage out of control. I've worked with many people who were paralyzed by fear. You may have a friend like this. Sometimes she's afraid to make a decision, risk another's disapproval, or take a stand. She may be afraid that others don't like her. And even worse, she's afraid to break out of this pattern she is trapped in.

This discussion on trauma is basic and oversimplified. It's informational. But you need information to understand what your friend is experiencing. The information is meant to alert you to the fact that trauma exists and is perhaps closer to you than you realize. If you identify yourself as one of those experiencing any degree of PTSD, or you know someone who fits the characteristics, remember this:

1. *Being traumatized is not incurable*; recovery is possible, but it is

a slow process. Your friend needs to hear this.

2. *Your friend will need to work with a professional,* someone who is equipped to assist those experiencing trauma. This could be a highly trained minister, chaplain, or therapist.

3. *Control can come through understanding.* The more you learn about trauma for yourself or for others, the more you and the other person will feel in control of life.

THE OTHER SIDE OF TRAUMA

Keep in mind that there is another side to trauma. The current research on those who have been traumatized indicates the majority of victims say they eventually benefited from the trauma in some way. And these are people who experienced as much pain as those who have never fully recovered. How did they benefit? There was a change of values, a greater appreciation for life, a deepening of spiritual beliefs, a feeling of greater strength, and building stronger relationships.

"The most important element in recovering is to remain connected to other people."[5] Your friend needs other people to walk with her at this time of life more than any other.

One of the best steps for your friend to take is to stop seeing herself as a person who is diseased or deficient. Your friend is not abnormal because of her trauma symptoms; it is the *event* she experienced that was abnormal. The event was so out of the ordinary that it overwhelmed her, as it would anyone—including you.[6]

THREE STAGES OF RECOVERY

How will your friend recover? She will need to go through the *thinking stage,* the *emotional stage,* and the *mastery stage.* The *thinking stage* involves fully facing her trauma, remembering it, and even reconstructing it mentally. This isn't a matter of dwelling in the past but of taking fragmented and disconnected memories and pulling them together so that your friend can make sense of the present. Sometimes this stage involves talking with others (like you), re-creating the scene, or reading any written accounts of it. When this is accomplished she will be able to view what happened from a new perspective—an objective view rather than a judgmental view.[7] It'll be like reading a newspaper account.

In the thinking stage she needs to look at what happened to her as a detached observer (even though it may be difficult) rather than as an emotionally involved participant. If she's able to work through this stage, she will acquire a new assessment of what her real choices were during the traumatic experience. She'll have a better under-standing of how the event has impacted the totality of her life and will be able to reduce the self-blame that most experience. Finally, she'll gain a clearer understanding of who or what she may be angry at.[8] And anger is usually present. And it's all right.

The thinking stage deals with the mental area, but healing and recovery must also involve the *emotional* level. This second stage will necessitate dealing with any of the feelings she may have repressed because of the trauma. Feelings hurt. Those emotions must be expressed on the gut level. This isn't easy; many people have a fear of feeling worse and losing control. Your friend doesn't have to act on the feelings, nor will they take over her life. But she does need to face them. And these could include anger, anxiety, grief, fear, sadness . . . the list goes on and on.[9] How can you help? If your friend shows signs of anger, have her draw her anger, whisper in as loud a voice as pos-sible, give it other names, write a letter to her anger, or have her anger write one back to her. The possibilities are endless.

The final stage is the *mastery stage*. This is when your friend finds new meaning through what she's experienced, and her perspective becomes that of a survivor rather than a victim. Who has greatest potential to become a survivor? A person who has a relationship with Jesus Christ and a biblical worldview.

Mastering the trauma involves making her own decisions instead of allowing experiences, memories, or other people to make decisions for her. This is a time of growth, change, and new direction in her life. What anyone learns because of a trauma probably could not have been learned any other way. Look at what Scripture says about this:

> Blessed be the God and Father of our Lord Jesus Christ, the Father of mercies and God of all comfort; who comforts us in all our affliction so that we may be able to comfort those who are in any affliction with the comfort with which we ourselves are comforted by God. For just as the sufferings of Christ are ours in abundance, so also our comfort is abundant through Christ. But if we are afflicted, it is for your comfort and salvation; or if we are comforted, it is for your comfort, which is effective in the patient enduring of the same sufferings which we also suffer. (2 Corinthians 1:3–6 NASB)

I've had people ask me, "How do I know I'm growing and getting better?" First, the person has to develop a new way of looking at the progress. It may be slow. There may be regression. She needs to focus on the improvements rather than the times she feels stuck. One man told me that he rated his progress each month on a scale of one to ten, as well as his entire journey of healing up to that point. That helped him understand his own progress.

How can a person tell if she's progressing and moving ahead? Symptoms become less frequent, and the struggle with fear will become less intense. One of the fears that is so disheartening is the fear of going crazy or insane. This fear will also diminish.

However, there will be times when the only way to get rid of anger and feelings of revenge is to face the fact that nothing can be done to change what happened or prevent a similar occurrence in the future. Then the next step is to begin to give up a portion of her anger or resentment each day. It's like saying, "All right, today I'm giving up 5 percent of my anger and tomorrow another 5 percent."

As your friend moves through her journey to recovery, the rigidity that helped her cope will diminish. She'll gradually discover the value of flexibility and spontaneity to the degree that she's comfortable with it, based on her unique personality.

One of the delights of recovery is developing a new appreciation of life. Your friend will begin to see what she wasn't seeing before, to hear what she couldn't hear before, to taste what was tasteless before.

Some people rediscover their sense of humor and all its healing properties.

They'll discover a new and deeper sense of empathy for the wounded around them. A trauma survivor can actually become a wounded healer and have a greater compassion for others. The verse that says, "Weep with those who weep," takes on a new meaning (Romans 12:15 NASB).[10]

People who are recovering commonly struggle to see and measure their progress. For years I've had counselees keep a daily or weekly journal in which they explicitly write out what they are experiencing or feeling. Some keep a time line of recovery. Some do both. Over time this makes a person aware, in a tangible way, of his or her recovery.

A recovery time line is a simple way to record the peaks and valleys of the recovery process. Plot the days at the bottom of a paper and a scale of 1 to 10 on the left. At the end of each day, the person indicates where she is for that day. This might go on for months or years, but over time growth is discovered.

When your friend has experienced trauma, sometimes that's all she remembers. What would happen if she were able to leapfrog over that event back to what her life was like before the trauma? We call this "looking at your life as it was." What was her life like? What did she do each day? You could assist her in answering the following questions to help recapture time before the trauma. The questions include:

What was your biggest struggle then?
What fulfilled you?
What did you enjoy the most?
What did you look like then? (It helps to be very specific about this. Sometimes pictures and videos help the process.)
Who were your friends?
What did you like and not like about yourself?
Who did you get along with?
Who didn't you get along with?
What did you believe about God then?
What were your Christian practices, such as prayer?
What were your beliefs about life then?
What were you realistic about? Naïve about?
What did you want out of life then?
What were your goals or dreams for yourself then?
What are your goals or dreams for yourself now?
What would you like to be different now?

As your friend looks at what she wrote, help her decide what is different now. What alternatives can she think of to make her life more the way she wants it to be? Have her make a list of all the things she would like to happen now (dream big), and then check off what possibly could happen if she chose to pursue this avenue. What would keep her from growing and changing? For many, it's the lack of a plan. Dreams can fade without a plan. It's helpful to have someone assist with these questions; you might be that person for your friend.

Overcoming trauma is a process—a journey. But we don't travel the journey alone; the Lord is with us.

The Spirit of the Sovereign Lord is on me, because the Lord has anointed me to preach good news to the poor. He has sent me to bind up the brokenhearted, to proclaim freedom for the captives and release for the prisoners. (Isaiah 61:1)

When Jesus spoke again to the people, he said, "I am the light of the world. Whoever follows me will never walk in darkness, but will have the light of life" (John 8:12).

You, O Lord, keep my lamp burning; my God turns my darkness into light. (Psalm 18:28)

Remember—you *can* help. Be there for your friend. Listen with your heart, reach out with the hands of Jesus, and pray.[11]

Chapter 8

HELPING A FRIEND IN A CRISIS OR TRAUMA

WHEN A FRIEND CALLS AND NEEDS your help there is a set way to respond. Remember that you are helping as a compassionate friend. In some cases he may need professional help, but you may be the first one he reaches out to so you need to stand in the gap for him. Keeping this in mind will encourage you to pray more and to be dependent on the leading of the Holy Spirit for listening, words, and direction. Some of the same suggestions apply whether your friend has experienced a crisis or a trauma.

As you are gathering information from his story and answers to your questions, you're seeking to discover the following: (1) Which issues in your friend's life need to be attended to immediately? and (2) Which issues can be postponed until later? Help him make this determination, because so often people in crisis are not aware of what can wait and what must be handled at once. Sometimes it's as simple as getting him some food and rest. As you work more in crisis situations, you will discover that you seldom have to conduct a question-by-question approach to derive critical information. Your friend will volunteer most of it. But as you discuss the situation with him, *be sure to keep the questions in this chapter in mind.*[1]

Be aware of your friend's level of alertness and communication capabilities. Attempt to identify the cause of the crisis with questions such as, "Tell me what has happened to make you so upset," or "Can you tell me the reason you're so upset? I'd like to hear what you have to say." *Telling his story as he experienced it is foundational.* Don't start with feelings, which is what many people are prone to do. "Tell me how you're feeling" is *not* the starting point.

Those in a crisis sometimes have difficulty stating clearly what they want to say. When this occurs, you'll need to be extremely patient. Any verbal or nonverbal indication of impatience, discomfort, or urging your friend to hurry is counterproductive. Allow for pauses and remain calm. Remember that especially during the impact phase of the crisis there is a stage of confusion and disorientation, and the mental processes are not functioning as they normally would. Some of the pain is so extreme that the words will not come easily. And in some cases, there may be no words to describe your friend's experience.

Sometimes what you're hearing doesn't sound rational, and it may not be. How do you handle irrationality that you cannot stop? Look at your own need to be in control as well as helping others to feel better. Helping a devastated friend will tap your energy and push your ability to be flexible to the wall. It's common as well as all right to think *Will this ever end?* or *I don't know how much more of this I can take.* Just as your friend's reactions are normal, so are your own.

HELP FOR YOU, THE CAREGIVER

Before becoming significantly involved in helping others, you need to be aware of a problem that none of us are immune to. It has different names, such as *compassion fatigue, helper shutdown,* or *helper burnout,* and it can happen to doctors, nurses, counselors, rescue workers, or anyone involved in helping others. It seems to be a case of emotional contagion—you end up catching the disorder of the person or people you are helping. You become emotionally drained by caring too much. It's stress from wanting to help another person. When you minister to a friend, he may leave feeling better, but you're absorbed in his problems emotionally as well as mentally.

This can happen for several reasons. It can be an overload if you're helping a number of hurting individuals at the same time. The desire to help others is good, but you need to realize not everyone will be helped and there are some who aren't willing to take steps to change. You may end up with what we call "mission failure" or "I didn't help them enough." You won't. The one bringing the changes is the Lord. We need to relinquish others to His care. Your value in helping others is to be there for them and follow the helpful guidelines, but don't evaluate your effectiveness on how well they respond.

As a counselor I've learned that sometimes you don't see the results of your efforts as people move on. If you are too empathetic and feel what your friend is feeling too much you will begin to carry his burdens around.

If you have unresolved trauma in your own life, be prepared to have it activated if you work with friends who have experienced trauma. What you hear may hit too close to home.

What will especially impact you is helping children who have experienced trauma. This affects even the most experienced professional helper.

What can you do? Make sure you maintain a balance in your life. You need to have times just for tending to and nurturing yourself through the Word, healthy friendships, exercise, recreation, devotional reading, laughter, and allowing others to care for you.

Sometimes you discover that helping certain friends is just too draining. You'll feel empty after every encounter and your friend may need assistance from someone other than you. Be aware of your thoughts. If you're constantly thinking about your friend's problems and you don't relinquish his issues to the Lord, you could end up in difficulty.

Two resources you may want to read and recommend to those you help are *Making Peace With Your Past*[2] and *Winning Over Your Emotions*.[3]

RESPONDING TO A FRIEND IN CRISIS

As you listen to your friend, notice if he's expressing any important themes. You can detect this either through statements being repeated or if your friend is speaking with great intensity. These are clues to the person's point of distress.

After your friend has described what's happened, you could ask, "What thoughts went through your mind at this time?" or "What did you think about when that occurred?" Since his thoughts are in such disarray right now, you're trying to help him reduce the clutter and cobwebs. As your friend begins to think a bit more clearly (and this will come and go) he feels a bit more in control. But remember that he may not remember all of what happened, and this can bother him. Details may be sketchy. You can reassure him that this is normal for what he's been through.

Eventually ask, "What was your reaction or response to this?" If you're talking with a man, use the words *response* and *reaction*, since many men don't relate to the word *feelings*.

On occasion you may need to channel the direction of the conversation. Some crisis situations need *immediate* action rather than tomorrow or next week. You can reinforce statements that are related to the crisis and avoid responding to unrelated topics, such as rambling statements that deal with the past or peripheral events. You might say, "What you have just said sounds important to you, and in the future we can talk about it. But right now, it doesn't seem directly related to your real concern. Let's come back to that." This process of focusing helps filter out any material that is irrelevant to the crisis but that the person may not realize is meaningless. A gentle supportive tone is very important.

If you're confused by what is said, don't hesitate to ask for clarification. When he's able to express the issues fairly clearly, help him to explore the alternatives available to deal with the situation. Ask questions such as "What else might be done at this time?" Discover what other support systems your friend has if you don't know—spouse, parents, friends, or fellow workers.

Anyone in a crisis will interpret his environment as something that's difficult to manage. He sees confusion and perhaps even chaos. Try to determine if you might be able to bring a greater sense of order to his environment. If you can assist in bringing a sense of calm, stability, and relief, believe me, this will be appreciated! Perhaps your friend needs to stay at a different location for a while. He may need some space and quiet, or even to be away from others who are attempting to help but actually add to the confusion by their inappropriate attempts.

As the person talks with you, assess what he's telling you and compare it to the problem as you see it. Remember, often a crisis is triggered by the person's *perception* of what has occurred. There may be times when you feel your friend is overreacting, but remember that what he is reacting to might not be the main problem. Some people fall apart over an insignificant occurrence that's really only a trigger mechanism. There may be a blocked or delayed response to another crucial problem.

For example, a mother seemed to be functioning quite well after a major accident that killed one person and critically injured her son. But while washing dishes in her kitchen, she dropped a plate and immediately fell apart. She alternated between hysterical weeping and intense anger. A relative visiting in the home couldn't understand this reaction to the simple breaking of a plate. The friend who worked with her later in the day, however, was able to bring all the factors together.

THE CAREGIVER'S ROLE

An often asked question is, "How do I know how much action to take?" A rule of thumb is this: only if circumstances severely limit your friend's ability to function do you take extensive action. And when you do, you want to move him to an independent role as soon as possible.

If the crisis is likely to result in danger to your friend or to others, if he's emotionally overwhelmed and has no capability to function or take care of himself, if he's on drugs or alcohol, or if he's injured, *then* you would take a more *directive role*.

When your friend isn't a danger to others or himself, when he's capable of making phone calls, running errands, driving, and caring for himself or others, your role is *facilitative*. The two of you may make the plans together, but your friend needs to carry out the plan. You may even want to work out a contract with him detailing how the plans are to be carried out. Does all this sound like what a counselor does? Yes, but it's quite structured and it isn't therapy.

Whether you are taking directive action or a facilitative role, *listening* and *encouraging* are primary tools.

Your advice should help your friend figure out his options. You might say, "You know, I am concerned about what's happening to you at this time. Let's consider doing this for now. . . ."

You can advise new approaches and actions. You can also advise a new way of thinking or looking at the situation. Often I have people come in with statements such as, "I'm cracking up," "I think I'm going crazy," "I must be the only person to feel this way," "Other people don't have this much pain, do they?" "I'm really a crummy Christian, aren't I?" "If I had more faith, I wouldn't be responding this way." What are these people really saying? What are they really feeling? They're saying, "I'm out of control. I'm afraid." They're trying to figure out what is happening to them, and this is their attempt to understand their predicament.

Here's your opportunity to offer your friend realistic reassurance with statements such as, "It's common to feel this way, but it's doubtful that you're going crazy. Your reaction and feelings are normal considering all that you have been experiencing." Or you might say, "With all you've been through, I'd be a bit concerned if you weren't reacting in some way." Helping him realize that his feelings and reactions are normal can be a source of relief.

Often I show the person I'm helping the crisis sequence chart described in chapter 5; this helps to relieve pressure.

Before you take action, ask yourself questions such as:

"Is this something my friend could do for himself?"

"What will this accomplish in the long run?"

"How long will I need to be involved in this way?"

"Are there any risks in doing this? If so, what are they?"

"How could my friend be helped in a different manner?"

Your friend's feeling of helplessness is strong during a crisis; you can counter this helpless feeling by encouraging him to create alternatives and take action. This will also help him operate from a position of strength rather than weakness. One way is to ask how he has handled previous difficulties. Once again, remember to have him— not you—do as much of the work as possible in order to build his self-esteem.

Coach him to consider the possibility that there are other alternatives. Some statements can be structured in a tentative, open-ended way: "Let's consider this possibility. What if you were to . . ." "What might happen if you would . . ." "Let's think of a person you feel is a real problem solver. What might that person do?" Be sure to help him anticipate any obstacles to implementing the plan. We cannot assume that he will follow through without first considering the obstacles.[4]

One way you can assist is by helping your friend avert a catastrophe and move toward a state of balance. If he's just lost his job he could, with your help, make a list of his qualifications, abilities, and job experiences. Just the simple task of completing some action can provide a sense of relief.

Since anyone in crisis or trauma feels hopeless, it's important to *foster hope and positive expectations*. Don't give false promises, but encourage him to solve his problems. Your belief in your friend's capabilities will be important. This is a time when he needs to borrow your hope and faith until his own returns. You expect the crisis to be resolved in some way at some time, and you expect him to work and be able to solve problems. It's your approach and interaction with the person that usually convey this rather than making blanket statements to him.

The problem-solving approach, rather than giving false reassurances, is a positive step. On occasion it's helpful to ask about past crises and upsets to discover how he handled them. If you are familiar with some of these, you could refer to his handling of them. This helps him see that he has been able to work through past problems, which can help in instilling hope for the current problem. Begin to help your friend set goals for the future if he is at that phase of the crisis sequence.

As his anxiety level drops, he'll see the situation in a more objective manner. When this occurs, he can reflect on what has happened and what is now occurring. Don't be surprised when laughter occurs. As there's a time to weep, there's also a time to laugh. We all look to humor to help us take a break from the heaviness of our loss or other tragedy. Many in the helping profession use what we call *gallows humor* to handle the pain and tragedy we see on a continued basis.

You can help your friend restore balance in several important ways. First, look at the information he's giving you about the situation. Does he see the complete picture or only selected aspects? Does he have all the facts? Is he distorting the situation because of his emotions or his own biases? Does he understand that certain responses and feelings are normal during a time of crisis?

Asking pertinent questions and prodding for informational answers can help. (1) You can help to fill in some of his informational gaps, and (2) his fears and concerns can be diminished as he receives accurate information. Both steps help to restore equilibrium.

How well does your friend grasp the choice of action open to him in light of the recent changes in his life (such as the loss of a job or a spouse)? What options are open to him (such as caring for the children if a spouse has died or left)? Anyone in this situation needs help considering the choices and the consequences of decisions both to himself and others who may be involved. Examining choices and consequences and then selecting a path enables him to cope now as well as in future situations.

As your friend gains greater strength and capability, he'll be able to examine his part in the situation and how he is responding with feelings and behavior.

PROVIDING SUPPORT

What else can you do? You can provide support. One of the reasons a problem develops into a crisis is the lack of an adequate social support system. Intervention in a crisis involves giving support, and initially *you* may be the only one giving it. Just being available to talk by phone is a source of support.

The knowledge that you are praying for your friend each day and are available to pray with him over the phone is a source of support. Don't be surprised by a number of "urgent" calls during the early steps of a crisis. These need to be returned promptly and often. Their purpose is to gain support just through simple contact with you.

It's important to return calls promptly, but that's not the same as immediately. If you drop everything you're doing to call back, a dependency relationship could be encouraged and your day ends up in chaos. If a half hour goes by, your friend has the opportunity to do some thinking on his own. He may calm down, and by the time you talk to him, the problem or issue is no longer critical. This is important, because it takes you out of the magical miracle-worker role.

Those in crisis need the assurance that they can call you at any time and you will be willing to talk to them for a few minutes. Will this work for you? What about your own work and family? You may decide your friend needs to see a trained pastor or counselor while you play a secondary supportive role. But even if you tell him to call anytime, he will still struggle with whether or not to call. If you don't let him know he can call, his struggle could be intensified and therefore add to his crisis condition.

At some point you may need to set some limits on the phone calls as your friend becomes better able to handle his life. That's one way to express the limits! Because you can tell he's better able to handle what's occurring, you want him to exercise his capabilities a bit more.

The best way of supporting your friend is to expand his support system as soon as possible. This reduces demands on you. It helps him through the immediate crisis, and it can help to prevent a crisis in the future.

Try to determine what type of support system your friend has. Does he have any relatives or friends in the area? Are they functional or will they drag your friend down? These need to be people who replenish rather than deplete. Whom has he told about his difficulty? Learn about the helping agencies—such as those that provide financial or housing support or a suicide prevention center—in your area so you can direct him toward such help when needed. Neighbors and friends can provide baby-sitting or transportation. People from the church can provide cooked meals over a period of time. Try to determine whom he can draw on and what they can do to reduce the pressures upon him during his crisis. This is a very practical way of helping.

Be sure you give some specific guidance to the support people. They're not to give a lot of verbal advice, which may be well intended but unnecessary. Sometimes you need to give some direct guidance even though it seems uncomfortable. But whoever said helping a friend is easy? It costs in time and energy. But it's worth it. After all, it's a calling and a privilege.

RECOMMENDED READING

When Your World Falls Apart: Life Lessons From a Ground Zero Chaplain, Mike Macintosh (Victor Books, 2002)
Will My Life Ever Be the Same, H. Norman Wright (Harvest House, 2002)

Chapter 9

HELP! MY FRIEND IS DEPRESSED

I'M NOT SURE WHAT TO DO for this friend. Every time she calls she's either depressed or worried sick. I know she's been through a lot recently and I wish she'd get some help. I'm not sure what to say or do. I don't want to make the problem worse." Many of us find ourselves in this quandary at some time. You may be the first link in helping your friend find the help she needs.

Keep in mind that depression is a very normal response to losses and trauma.

If your friend is depressed, she desperately needs someone to help her. But she may not be able to communicate to you what she is experiencing. If you haven't felt hopeless and helpless yourself, it may not be easy for you to understand what she is going through. You may feel frustrated because of her inability to fully explain to you what she is experiencing. You'll also be frustrated because of wanting to help but not knowing what to do.

Picture the depressed person down in a deep pit. The pit is dark, cold, and very isolated; it is frighteningly lonely. On all sides there are only rocky walls; there are no handholds or solid footholds that would provide a way to climb up and out. The person in the pit is completely helpless and easily becomes resigned to days of darkness and despair. There seems to be no way of escape.

This is how your friend feels when she has sunk to the depths of depression. She feels overwhelmed and imprisoned by nagging but deadly feelings of worthlessness, fear, and self-blame. Concerned friends or family members stand above on the edge of the pit, yearning to help. Even so, it's very hard to call for help from the paralyzing helplessness of depression. Sometimes it's difficult to admit to others that you're even down there.[1]

As you offer help to your depressed friend, pray for understanding and patience. You'll need an abundance of both. Your offer to help may be rejected at first, and it could be some time before it is accepted. You can't just go down into the pit, grab her, and hoist her to the top. You'd like to, but it doesn't work that way. Your friend must be willing to trust God and other people. She must decide to begin to climb out of the pit herself. Your encouragement will be like a ladder placed inside the pit, and it may give her the motivation and hope to begin the climb.

Picture yourself at the top of the pit looking down. There's a balcony at the top, and you're leaning over the balcony railing cheering her on in her climb up the ladder. Your belief in her ability to climb out may be the source of strength that she needs. When people have no hope, we need to loan them our hope until they can regain their own.

This is also a time to help the depressed person capture the hope of the Word of God as expressed in Isaiah 40:28–31:

> Do you not know? Have you not heard?
> The Everlasting God, the Lord, the Creator of the ends of the
>   earth
> Does not become weary or tired.
> His understanding is inscrutable.
> He gives strength to the weary,
> And to him who lacks might He increases power.
> Though youths grow weary and tired,

And vigorous young men stumble badly,
Yet those who wait for the Lord
Will gain new strength;
They will mount up with wings like eagles,
They will run and not get tired,
They will walk and not become weary. (NASB)

If you're around a depressed person you will have to protect two people—the depressed person and yourself. Why? Because the depression will affect both of you. You're dealing with someone who is very sensitive, and you must exhibit a certain sensitivity toward her. You're a giver and your friend is a receiver, but you may feel angry and irritated at the way she is acting, which in turn can make you feel guilty for feeling that way. Because of your anger you may respond in ways you do not want to respond, and this tends to increase your anger. Your friend will sense this and feel even worse because she feels that she is a burden on you. In time you may feel drained.

If you're depressed yourself, you shouldn't attempt to help someone else with her depression or you'll find yourself feeling overwhelmed. Your relationship could experience a strain as well.

What can you say to a friend or relative who is going through depression? Simply, "I care for you and I am available. I want to help you and be with you." Put your arm around the person and hold his or her hand. There is healing in our physical touch. A touch on the shoulder, a pat on the back, or holding the arm all convey acceptance and the feeling, "I am with you." Be honest and tell the person, "I don't understand all that you are going through, but I am trying to understand. I will be here to help you."

We may never know what our praying for and with a depressed friend will do for her. In a time of depression when our friend has lost hope, we need to lend her our hope to carry her through. When she has lost faith, she needs our faith to sustain her until hers is recovered.

PRACTICAL GUIDELINES TO FOLLOW

Most people don't know what to do for a depressed person. Here are some practical guidelines to follow. How closely you follow these will depend upon the intensity and duration of the person's depression. If she is depressed for only a few hours or a day or two, or if she is feeling down but is functioning, not all the suggestions apply. But if the depression has lasted for weeks or months and she is dragging, not functioning, not eating, and/or not sleeping, apply the appropriate measures.

1. Understanding the causes and symptoms of depression is the first step toward helping. If your friend is so depressed that she just stares, ignores greetings, or turns away from you, remember that she doesn't want to act that way. In depression, the person loses the ability to govern her thinking and her emotions. If she is severely depressed she cannot control herself any more than you could walk a straight line after twirling yourself around in a tight circle twenty-five times. If you understand how the person is feeling and why she is acting the way she is, if you understand that her behavior is the normal behavior of a depressed person, then you can be in better control of your own responses and you will be better able to help her.

2. Watch out for suicide. Any hint or statement or allusion to suicide should be talked about. I know it's difficult to accept that your friend would ever consider this, but it does happen. It has to me. It helps the depressed person to bring it out into the open and talk about it. Then she knows that other people are aware and can be called upon for help and support. Ask her to tell you about her suicidal thoughts or plans. Remember too that women make many more attempts at suicide than men, but men are more likely to succeed. A divorced man over the age of forty is at the highest risk. Any person who is so depressed that she talks about the utter hopelessness of the future might be considering suicide.

3. Encourage your depressed friend to see a doctor. Your family physician may be able to help or may recommend someone who can. The time factor is very important. Don't let depression go on and on. Even if your friend keeps putting you off and refusing to go, make the arrangements, guide her firmly into the car, and go!

4. To help you identify the extent of your friend's depression use the diagram below. Show your friend the diagram and ask her to indicate where she is at this moment with her depression:

0		5		10
Not depressed at all	A few clouds	It's getting overcast	The sky is darker	Heavy depression

If you are helping your friend over a period of time you could have her evaluate her depression each month and note her progress.

5. Give your friend your full support. Her entire family ought to be made aware of the situation and given instruction as to their responses. Confrontations with the depressed person should be suspended until she achieves greater stability. Tell the family not to attack your depressed friend, not to bring up her failures, not to come down hard on her, but to ask her to do things that she is capable of doing while she is depressed.

6. Don't avoid a depressed friend. This further isolates her and could make her worse. Some might avoid her because they experience guilt over her depression, thinking that they may be the cause. Remember that one person may contribute to another's problem from time to time, but no one is responsible for another person's unhappiness.

7. Understand that a depressed friend really hurts. Don't suggest that she doesn't really feel bad or that she is just trying to get your sympathy. Don't tell her that all she has to do is "just pray about it and read the Word more" and that will solve everything. Often a depressed person chooses portions of the Scripture that reinforce her

feelings of loss and unworthiness. Any Scriptures given to a depressed person must be selected with care.

8. Empathize, rather than sympathize, with your friend. Sympathy can only reinforce the feelings of hopelessness. It may make her feel more helpless and may lower her already low self-esteem. Statements such as "It's so awful that you are depressed," "You must feel miserable," or "How could this ever happen?" rarely help.

Remember that any depressed person's complaints are expressions of emotional pain. Don't get embroiled in a battle over the content of the statement. Stick with her feelings. Here are some specific guidelines:

- "I'm all alone."
  Don't say: "No you're not! I'm sitting here with you right now. Doesn't my friendship mean anything?"
  Do say: "I know that you're feeling alone right now. Is there anything I can do to help? I'm glad to just be with you. Together we'll get through this lonely feeling."
- "Why bother? Life isn't worth living. There's no point in going on."
  Don't say: "How can you think that? You have two beautiful children and a great job. You have everything to live for."
  Do say: "I know it feels that way to you right now, but I want you to know that you matter to many. You will get through this hopeless feeling."
- "I'm dragging everyone else down with me."
  Don't say: "No you're not. You see? I'm fine. I had a good day today. And besides, I'm doing everything in the world to help you."
  Do say: "I know it feels that way right now. And yes, at times it is difficult for others, but everyone will get though this burdened feeling together."

- "What would it be like if I weren't here anymore?"
  Don't say: "Don't talk crazy! What's wrong with you?"
  Do say: "There are many, including me, who would miss you terribly. You're important to so many. We'll all help and get through this together."
- "I'm expendable."
  Don't say: "If you felt better about yourself, you wouldn't say stupid things like that."
  Do say: "I know you're feeling worthless right now, but we'll get through this."
- "Nothing I do is any good. I'll never amount to anything."
  Don't say: "What are you saying? You're a highly respected engineer! You're blowing everything out of proportion."
  Do say: "I know it's upsetting when things don't work out the way you want them to. Failure feelings are really painful. We'll get through this together."
- "How long am I going to feel this way? It feels as if I'll never get better."
  Don't say: "C'mon, nothing lasts forever. You know better than that."
  Do say: "I know it's scary to be in so much pain. Feelings come and go. We'll get through this together."[2]

9. If your friend loses interest in activities she normally enjoys, you can gently remind her of the past enjoyment that she derived from the activities and then firmly encourage her to become involved. Don't ask her if she would like to, as she might not know or may not care to respond. Don't get angry and say, "You're going with me because I'm sick and tired of you sitting around feeling sorry for yourself." You could say, "I know that you haven't felt well in the past, but I feel that you are entitled to some enjoyment. I think you might like this once we get started. And I would like to share this activity with you."

Or perhaps you call to let her know what time the concert or activity begins. "I'm going shopping. I'd like to have someone with me, and you know that I rely upon your advice." Any activity such as window-shopping, a social event, or calling on others can be used. By getting involved, the person begins to break the destructive behavior patterns, and this helps her gain energy and motivation.

One of the best things to do is to keep your friend busy. Physical activity in severe depression can be more beneficial than mental activity. Her entire day might be scheduled for her. The activities planned should be those that she has enjoyed in the past, with all preparations made in detail.

10. If your friend begins to let her appearance go, don't hint about the situation. Openly, clearly, and explicitly tell her that she will enjoy fixing herself up and perhaps will feel better for it.

11. Loss of confidence and self-esteem is common in depression. Don't ever kid or tease or lecture her about her lack of confidence. And don't ignore it; it must be faced. In reactivating self-esteem, help the person see the illogic of her self-disparagement, but don't do it by berating or arguing. Look for past accomplishments in her life and get her to focus upon what she was able to accomplish prior to the onset of the depression. At this point you are trying to overcome her helplessness.

Don't join in the self-pity, but respond by saying, "Perhaps you can't do some things the way you did before, but let's talk about the things you still do well. What do you think they are?" If she says, "I can't do anything," gently name some things she can do, or draw them out of her. Be persistent and steady in your responses. Remember that at this point you have more control over your emotional responses than she has over hers.

By following these principles, it is possible for us to fulfill the biblical teaching on giving empathy and encouragement to one another. Galatians 6:1 says, "Brethren, if any person is overtaken in misconduct or sin of any sort, you who are spiritual [who are responsive to and controlled by the Spirit] should set him right and restore and reinstate him, without any sense of superiority and with all gentleness, keeping an attentive eye on yourself, lest you should be tempted also" (AMP). And 1 Thessalonians 5:14 says: "And we earnestly beseech you, brethren, admonish (warn and seriously advise) those who are out of line [the loafers, the disorderly, and the unruly]; encourage the timid and fainthearted, help and give your support to the weak souls, [and] be very patient with everybody [always keeping your temper]" (AMP).

There will be times when a friend is struggling with worry. In fact, it helps to ask, "Do you have a tendency to worry?" Most will say, "Oh, yes," or "It's a constant battle." (To help your friend with worry, read chapters 1–3 of my book *Winning Over Your Emotions*.)

Share the following suggestions with a friend (and they *do* work).

Read Psalm 37:1–7 aloud to your friend. You might share the following: Psalm 37:1 begins, "Do not fret," and those words are repeated later in the psalm. The dictionary defines "fret" as "to eat away, gnaw, gall, vex, worry, agitate, wear away."

In addition to telling us not to fret, Psalm 37 gives us positive substitutes for worry. First it says, "Trust (lean on, rely on, and be confident) in the Lord" (v. 3, AMP). Trust is a matter of not attempting to live an independent life or to cope with difficulties alone. It means going to a greater source for strength.

Second, verse four says, "Delight yourself also in the Lord" (AMP). To delight means to rejoice in God and what He has done for us, to let God supply the joy for our life.

Third, verse 5 says, "Commit your way to the Lord" (AMP). Commitment is a definite act of the will, and it involves releasing our worries and anxieties to the Lord.

And fourth, we are to "rest in the Lord; wait for Him" (verse 7 AMP). This means to submit in silence to what He ordains, and to be ready and expectant for what He is going to do in our life.[3]

Ask your friend to read these passages out loud several times a day as a reminder. Also ask what would assist her in applying each principle.

The next suggestion is a bit different: Say to your friend, "Tomorrow when you begin to worry about something, instead of worrying at that moment, write down what you're worried about on an index card and keep the card in your pocket. Each time a worry pops up, write it on the card, but don't worry about it yet. Then about 4 P.M., go into a room where you can be alone. Sit down, take out the card, and worry about those items as intensely as you can for thirty minutes. Start the next day with a new blank card and do the same thing."[4]

The most helpful approach I've learned over the years is the "Stop/Think" approach: Suggest to your friend that she take a blank index card and on one side write the word STOP in large, bold letters. On the other side write the complete text of Philippians 4:6–9. It's interesting to note that God says *He* will guard our hearts, but *we* are to guide our minds. Ask her to keep the card with her at all times. Whenever she is alone and begins to worry, take the card out, hold the STOP side in front of her, and say aloud "Stop!" twice with emphasis. Then suggest she turn the card over and read the Scripture passage aloud twice with emphasis.

This passage states:

> Don't worry about anything; instead pray about everything; tell God your needs, and don't forget to thank him for his answers. If you do this, you will experience God's peace, which is far more wonderful than the human mind can understand. His peace will keep your thoughts and your hearts quiet and at rest as you trust in Christ Jesus. And now, brothers, as I close this letter, let me say this one more thing: Fix your thoughts on what is true and good and right. Think about things that are pure and lovely, and dwell

on the fine, good things in others. Think about all you can praise God for and be glad about. Keep putting into practice all you learned from me and saw me doing, and the God of peace will be with you. (TLB)

Taking the card out interrupts her thought pattern of worry. Saying the word *Stop*! further breaks her automatic habit pattern of worry. Then reading the Word of God aloud becomes the positive substitute for worry. If she is in a group of people and begins to worry, she should follow the same procedure, only silently. It may sound different, but this has worked for thousands.

RESOURCES

Dark Clouds, Silver Linings, Archibald Hart (Focus on the Family, 1993)

When Feeling Bad Is Good, Ellen McGraw (Henry Holt, 1992)

When the Blues Won't Go Away, New Approaches to Dysthmic Disorder and Other Forms of Chronic Low-Grade Depression, Robert Hirschfield, M.D. (MacMillan, 1991)

Winning Over Your Emotions, H. Norman Wright (Harvest House, 1998)

Why Am I Depressed, Brenda Poinsett (NavPress, 1996)

Chapter 10

SAY IT IN WRITING

IF THERE IS ANYTHING THAT HELPS a hurting person more than spoken words it is written words. I know. Following the death of our son we received so many written expressions of comfort. And this went on for six or seven years—that's what helped so much. While *we* continued to receive written words of comfort, most people don't. We were fortunate.

Most who are hurting receive an abundance of cards and notes at first, during a time when their pain is so great the words of comfort may not register as much as they would later on. Write reminders on your calendar to send notes every three to four months for at least two years. All it takes is one person doing this; your act of caring sends the message, "Your loss is not forgotten." And letters and cards are not limited to a death. They can be for any loss.

Perhaps the most important part of sending a note is to put it in your own handwriting. A typed note or one purchased that you only sign doesn't convey the same message as one in your own handwriting. Time after time I've heard people comment on how meaningful the handwritten notes were. This act simply conveys how much you care for your hurting friend. Writing letters and notes to a hurting friend is not easy. In fact, for many the most challenging letter to write is a letter of condolence. How can you craft a simple expression of words on a page that can penetrate the pain of loss and grief and bring support and care to a friend's heart and mind? Sometimes the written word is heard more than the spoken word. Many letters that you write will be kept and reread for years.

You may think, *I just don't know what to say in a letter*. Most of us don't. It's a struggle. It's uncomfortable. We grope. We don't want to be superficial or stilted in our expression. So it's easy to postpone writing to the extent we never do it, even though we wanted to reach out in this way.

Listen to your feelings of compassion and care. Your task is to translate them into words. Your words acknowledge your friend's loss and to some degree you are sharing their pain.

"I don't know how to put what I'm feeling into words." That's all right. Few of us do. One of the easiest ways if you're stuck is to go to a store and select several appropriate condolence cards. Then simply write on your own card or stationery what's written on the purchased card. You can change the wording to make it sound like you. Someone else's words can stimulate your own thoughts. There will be several examples in this chapter that you can use to help you create your own expressions.

GUIDELINES FOR CREATING A CONDOLENCE LETTER OR CARD

The following can give you some structure, but these are just suggestions. You can change any of them to make your expressions more appropriate to the loss your friend has experienced.

The first component of a letter is to acknowledge the loss. If someone other than your friend informed you, let him know how you learned about his loss. It's all right to express your feelings about hearing of the loss. You can say you were shocked or stunned or taken back by the news. If the loss was a person, mention him by name. This can apply to a death, a divorce, or the breakup of a relationship.

Dear _____,

I was taken back today when John called to tell me that your father had died. It seemed so sudden and must have been a shock to you.

Express your concern. Let your friend know that you care and in some way you connect with his sense of loss. If you know the person who died (or left or otherwise was involved in the loss for your friend), share your sadness. When you do this it lets your friend know he's not alone with his feelings. And use the appropriate words. If it was a death, use the word. If it was a betrayal or a suicide, use those words.

It's hard to find the words to convey my love and concern for you over the untimely death of your father. I wish I could help fill that empty spot you have in your life at this time. I miss him too, as well as the ongoing stories you always recount to me. Those are a loss as well.

It helps to make note of special qualities of the person who died. This can be done whether you knew him personally or just through the stories of your friend. Acknowledge the attributes that you felt were positive—personality or the ways he related to others, for example. In doing this, you're reminding your friend that the person he lost made a contribution and was appreciated.

I remember the times I spent time with you and your father. He was a gracious man and showed interest in what I was involved in. He made me feel a part of your family. And he shared so well for a man! You and I have joked about that before!

It helps to share a special memory you have of the one who died. This can help your friend since his shock and grief have short-circuited his ability to remember details. When you share your memory tell what made it special to you. It could be serious or humorous.

> I remember one time when you invited me to a barbecue. Remember what your dad did to those porterhouse steaks? They were turned into charcoal when he got distracted. His sense of humor and willingness to go buy some more instead of getting upset impressed me so much. He really was special.

In addition to memories, it's helpful to mention special qualities about your friend. This is a time when he is so overwhelmed and nonfunctional that he may question his own capabilities. "How will I ever get through this? How will I ever survive?" are common expressions. Your friend needs your reassurance, your encouragement, and your confidence. You need to loan him your faith and hope since his own may have disappeared at this time. You can see what he cannot see at this time in his life. Bring out any traits that helped him deal with past adversities. And if you can remember any words or affirmations the deceased made about your friend, he needs to hear those now.

> This is going to be a difficult journey for you. It's not the first one you've been on. I've seen your strength and determination in adversity before. I remember your dad saying you were not only a survivor but a person who could take difficult times and use them not only for your growth but to bless others. In time this will occur again.

Part of your letter will be to offer assistance to your friend if you're able to do so. But whatever you offer, be sure you can follow through. Don't say, "Let me know if there's anything I can do." It's hard for your friend to think let alone ask for help. Take the lead and suggest two or three specific tasks that you could do, such as shopping, running errands, cleaning, or making phone calls, for example.

I want to help you in the best way possible. I have some ideas so I'll call Saturday after you've had some time and we can talk about them at that time.[1]

When you close your letter do so with a thoughtful word or phrase. This is another time to reflect your feelings. There are many expressions to use:

My affectionate respects to you and yours.
Our love is with you always.
You are in my thoughts and prayers.
You know you have my deepest sympathy and my love and friendship always.
My heart and my tears are with you.
We share in your grief and send you our love.
We offer our affectionate sympathy and many beautiful memories.
My thoughts are with you now, and I send you my deepest sympathy.
We all join in sending you our heartfelt love.[2]

What about sharing your own grief experiences? This can be done if you've had a similar loss experience, but don't compare the two. The worst and most anger-producing phrase we can use is, "I know (understand) exactly how you feel." No you don't. None of us do since grief and loss are so very personal. You could, however, share the depth of your pain and how you survived.

Future notes don't have to be long. They can be brief and to the point.

Hi, I was having my prayer time and your face came to mind. How are you *really* doing today? Hope you're eating and sleeping. I'll call for a breakfast. Love you.

SHARE THE WORD OF GOD

When you find yourself struggling with what to say, Scripture verses, including the following, can be helpful:

The eternal God is your Refuge, And underneath are the ever-lasting arms. (Deuteronomy 33:27 TLB)

When you go through deep waters and great trouble, I will be with you. When you go through rivers of difficulty, you will not drown! When you walk through the fire of oppression, you will not be burned up—the flames will not consume you. For I am the Lord your God, your Savior, the Holy One of Israel . . . Don't be afraid, for I am with you. (Isaiah 43:2–3, 5 TLB)

Let not your heart be troubled: ye believe in God . . . (John 14:1 KJV)

For I am persuaded, that neither death, nor life, nor angels, nor principalities, nor powers, nor things present, nor things to come, nor height, nor depth, nor any other creature, shall be able to separate us from the love of God, which is in Christ Jesus our Lord. (Romans 8:38–39 KJV)

Even though I walk through the valley of the shadow of death, I fear no evil; for Thou art with me; Thy rod and Thy staff, they comfort me. (Psalm 23:4 NASB)

God is our refuge and strength, A very present help in trouble. (Psalm 46:1 NASB)

He heals the brokenhearted. . . . (Psalm 147:3 NASB)

He hath said, I will never leave thee, nor forsake thee. (Hebrews 13:5 KJV)

Hope we have as an anchor of the soul, both sure and stedfast. (Hebrews 6:19 KJV)

Let not your heart be troubled; believe in God. (John 14:1 NASB)

Do not fear, for I am with you; do not be dismayed, for I am your God. I will strengthen you and help you; I will uphold you. (Isaiah 41:10)

Trust in the Lord with all thine heart; and lean not unto thine own understanding. In all thy ways acknowledge him, and he shall direct thy paths. (Proverbs 3:5–6 KJV)

When I pray, you answer me, and encourage me by giving me

the strength I need. (Psalm 138:3 TLB)

Be strong and courageous, do not be afraid . . . for the Lord your God is the one who goes with you. He will not fail you or forsake you. (Deuteronomy 31:6 NASB)

QUOTATIONS CAN HELP

Personal notes that include quotes, selected with sensitivity and the specific person in mind, take a little extra time and thought, but the healing effect they may have on a grief-stricken friend is well worth the effort. Sources for short, comforting quotes are almost limitless. One little book full of words of wisdom that will turn weakness into strength is *When Sorrow Comes,* by Robert Ozment. Here's a passage from that book that has been shared with those in despair:

I wish I had a magic word to wipe away your tears! I do not know any magic words, but I know a God who can heal you and I commend Him to you. Remember, the door of death is the only door that leads to the Father's house. He will be waiting there to greet and welcome His children.[3]

Peter Marshall, the legendary Scottish chaplain of the United States Senate in the late 1940s, died at age forty-six. Uncanny as it seems, he was reported to have spoken words befitting his own eulogy: "The measure of a life, after all, is not its duration, but its donation." When the death of a younger person occurs, these words may be appropriately incorporated into a personal note.

Quotes included in notes do not have to be spoken by famous people. The main criterion is that the quote is something that helps soothe the hurt caused by the death of a loved one.

An elderly widow shared a poem explaining that a friend copied it from a wooden decoupage at the home of another widow. These widows always pass this poem on with the hope that it will offer comfort to a new widow just as it spoke to them in their grief.

The lights are out
In the mansion of clay;
The curtains are drawn,
For the dweller's away;
He silently slipped
O'er the threshold by night,
To make his abode
In the City of Light.

One rancher in western Nebraska said the following poem was especially touching to him. A neighboring ranch family sent it to him, copied from a card they had received years before when the grandmother died.

In the Loss of Your Loved One
A chapter completed,
A page turned,
A life well lived,
A rest well earned.
May you find peace in
the knowledge that your
loved one has completed but
one chapter in the Book of
Eternal Life.

Helen Steiner Rice had a special gift of expressing emotions felt by grieving persons. Books of her poems are in most libraries.[4]

There are times when you can include poems, quotes, or Scripture. At other times prayers are appropriate to use in your letters or notes. Some examples are:

When the joy of living is lost, O God, and life becomes a long weariness, kindle again the light that has failed, and the love that will not let me go.

Lord, when sometimes my life in this world seems too much

to bear, help me to claim Your wonderful promise of victory over tears, death, sorrow and pain. I thank you that all things are made new through You and that I will share in Your kingdom.[5]

I am empty, Father. I am bitter, even toward You. I grieve, not only for the one I have lost, but for the loving part of myself that seems to have died as well. You, Who have at other times brought the dead back to life, revive my dead ability to love, to be close, to care about this world and those I know. I believe, I insist, that You can heal this mortal wound.[6] [7]

SAMPLE LETTERS

The following sample letters may assist you in creating your own. The first was read in the movie *Saving Private Ryan*:

Dear Madam,

I have been shown in the files of the War Department a statement of the Adjunct General of Massachusetts that you are the mother of five sons who have died gloriously on the field of battle. I feel how weak and fruitless must be any word of mine which should attempt to beguile you from the grief of a loss so overwhelming. But I cannot refrain from tendering you the consolation that may be found in the thanks of the republic they died to save. I pray that our Heavenly Father may assuage the anguish of your bereavement, and leave you only the cherished memory of the loved and lost, and the solemn pride that must be yours to have laid so costly a sacrifice upon the altar of freedom.

Yours very sincerely and respectfully,
A. Lincoln

Letter from an adult to an adult:

Dear Wendy and Spencer,

The news of your mother's death, while not unexpected, was nevertheless a blow. The final word is so definite always. I want to express my deep sympathy, but also, I feel a quiet understanding that your beloved mother—who suffered long—has finally found release. I can only imagine what the loss means to you and the rest of the family. You can all take great comfort from the fact that each and every one of you did everything possible—far beyond the call of duty—to make your mother's last troublesome days as easy for her as possible. She loved her family and knew that they loved her.

Dorothy's friends know how extraordinary a woman she was, as a wife, as a mother, as a friend, and as a co-worker. She has left her mark on us and we know that we have lost a great friend whose life was a pattern to guide us and an inspiration to live by. May God comfort you and ease your pain.[8]

Letter from an adult to a child:

Dear Jimmy,

Today I heard that your dad died just a few hours after the terrible accident. You feel awful and like your world turned upside down. All of us feel sad because your dad was such a neat man. He meant so much to us too.

Your life will be different in the next few weeks and months. Sometimes sadness makes us feel angry and confused. All of you in your family really need one another's love. It may be hard but it helps to talk about your sadness. It may help to draw or write about your feelings.

We all love you very much. I will call you real soon.

Letter upon the death of a spouse:

Dear Kim,

For the past day, my thoughts have been of nothing but you and the beautiful Julia. I don't know if there's anything that can be said to soften the pain of your grief just now, but my love, my unqualified friendship, and my prayers are with you.

Julia was such a vibrant spirit. Her exuberance made life around her a constant adventure. You joined her on that adventure with all your heart, whether sailing through the islands or sitting silently by a mountain stream. There was a sense among many who knew you that you each embraced fully the unknowable mystery that is life. I guess the mystery just gets deeper.

I'm reminded of a short piece by Henry Van Dyke. It's called "A Parable of Immortality":

"I am standing upon the seashore. A ship at my side spreads her white sails to the morning breeze and starts for the blue ocean. She is an object of beauty and strength, and I stand and watch until at last she hangs like a speck of white cloud just where the sea and sky come down to mingle with each other. Then someone at my side says, 'There she goes!'

"Gone where? Gone from my sight . . . that is all. She is just as large in mast and hull and spar as she was when she left my side and just as able to bear her load of living freight to the place of destination. Her diminished size is in me, not in her. And just at the moment when someone at my side says, 'There she goes!' there are other eyes watching her coming and other voices ready to take up the glad shout, 'Here she comes!' "

So, Alex, may the winds of life blow gently around you at this difficult time. I want to help in any way I'm able. I'll call Thursday.

In trust and friendship.[9]

If the loss was traumatic in some way you may struggle with what to say. Grief is intensified if there was no opportunity to say good-bye. No good-byes happen in the case of accidents, fatal heart attacks, homicide, suicide, etc. Often when a death occurs in this way there is an intensity of feelings that can include regrets, guilt, shame, anger, or rejection. There is the reaction of shock as well as the feeling of senselessness.

The following is a letter to the parents of a young woman who was murdered:

Dear Dr. and Mrs. Rodriguez,

It is with feelings of profound distress that we heard the very sad news of your daughter's death under such tragic circumstances. Her untimely passing is a most severe and grievous loss. There is no sense to it on Earth; we can only look to Jesus, Our Lord.

"Cast your cares on the Lord and he will sustain you" (Psalm 55:22).

We want to express our own deep sadness. Perhaps no words that we say will ease the pain, anguish, or emptiness that you feel in your hearts, but we want you to know that we will remember your daughter as a graceful, loving and open-hearted girl who brightened the neighborhood with her smile.

It may seem impossible now, but while nothing will ever bring Eileen back, we hope that one day you will find a source of comfort in beautiful memories of the years of joy God gave you together.

May God bless you and keep you.[10]

When our retarded son, Matthew, died in 1990 at the age of twenty-two (mentally he was about eighteen months old) we received an outpouring of cards and letters from scores of people. We kept them, as they contain so many significant memories. Since Matt lived at a special facility for the disabled the last eleven years of his life, some of the letters came from those who cared for him. Many contained a special experience they had with Matthew that we didn't know about. These experiences gave us new insights as well as memories about him, which have become very important. Even though you may think some experience might be trivial, to a bereaved parent it becomes special. I was comforted and felt loved by those who wrote. Their expressions assisted me with my own expression of grief, for I felt the loss more sharply each time I read a note.

In many of the letters the writers expressed their feelings and often similar experiences.

Let me close this chapter with portions of several letters we received:

Dear Norm and Joyce,

I sit here this evening thinking of you and crying for you. I know the pain you feel at this time and I hurt for you. Words do little to help right now but I hope you can take comfort in knowing that Matthew is with the Lord now and one day you'll be with him again at the feet of our Lord.

All of our thoughts, love and prayers are with you.

Dear Norm,

I just heard this morning of the death of your son, Matthew. I want you to know of our personal grieving for you and our prayers for you and your family during this time. My wife and I had a son who drowned almost eight years ago and so I can somewhat identify with the sense of loss that you are feeling. Please rest assured of our continued support and love for you as a Christian brother.

Dear Norm and Joyce,

Thank you for letting us know that Matthew has gone home to be with the Lord.

Our hearts are saddened for you as we know a little piece of your heart seems to be missing with Matthew's death—but we send our sympathy and love, hoping to help fill that hole a little bit.

Dear Dr. and Mrs. Wright,

I am so sorry to hear of the death of your son, Matthew. My wife and I lost a daughter about two years ago. And, my wife has a brother with Down's syndrome who's thirty-seven. So in a couple of respects I can identify to some degree with your grief.

Unfortunately, too many in the world don't understand the joy a mentally handicapped child can bring, even when the child has grown into adulthood. And so, I would imagine not everyone really knows how much you must be missing Matthew.

Dear Norm and Joyce,

You have been in our thoughts and prayers a great deal this week. We're praying you will feel God's peace and special care for you.

We have been thinking about Matthew, too—Remember the time, many years ago, when we Talbot students came to your home for a Christmas party. We met a tiny Matthew, just a few months old, and as far as any of us knew, a perfect baby. And now he is perfect!!

Chapter 11

PRAY FOR YOUR FRIEND

WITH THE RING OF THE PHONE one morning I found myself speaking to a thirty-two-year-old man who was concerned about his forthcoming marriage. As we talked he told me he wanted to marry this woman he had been going with for over a year. He had made a commitment and given her the ring; now fears stemming from his childhood had begun to emerge. (This is not an uncommon situation.)

We continued to talk about the marriage and the normal concerns that most individuals have concerning this major life step. "I feel I need prayer at this time," he concluded. "Would you seal our conversation with prayer?" And at that moment, distanced by many miles, yet very close because of the phone connection and our common relationship with Jesus Christ, I prayed for him. I asked for God's insight, direction, clarity of thought, leading, and peace to invade this brother's life.

We don't have to be face-to-face to minister to a friend in prayer. As we minister over the telephone to those who are close to us, our prayer draws them closer to relying upon the Lord instead of upon themselves or us.

As I get to know counselees in my office, I share with them during the first or second session that, as part of my counseling ministry, I will pray for them each day. And I tell them I would appreciate their letting me know from time to time what they would like me to pray about in their lives so that I can be sure to be current. Many of them are taken aback that someone would remember them in prayer. But over the years many counselees have said that knowing one person was praying for them kept them going.

I admit there are days when I do not pray as I have promised that I would. But I think that 80 percent of the time I am consistent in this practice and I let them know this.

Praying accomplishes several things. It releases our friend to God and it reminds us that we are not the ones who are the final resource in this life. We need the direct intervention of God in the life of our friend to guide, sustain, and comfort him. I've discovered that by keeping a list and praying for my counselees' specific concerns and issues, when they walk into my office I know what their concerns have been the week before. Praying is a reminder and reinforces their situation upon my mind.

Sometimes the counselee asks, "How did you remember what we discussed? I don't ever see you taking many notes." My answer is that prayer is a reminder.

There will be times when you are stumped, as I have been, and you won't know how to proceed or what to say. It is perfectly all right to admit that: "I'm not sure where to go next or what is more pressing. Let's just stop; I would like to ask God for guidance and insight for the direction needed at this time."

The core of helping others is prayer. But too little is said about prayer in counseling and too little is written about its use during the session and between sessions. This is not a chapter on what prayer is or how to pray according to this pattern or that pattern. Numerous books have been written on those topics. What I want to address is the use of prayer as a means of healing in the process of counseling.

SCRIPTURE AND PRAYER

The Scripture teaches that as we pray, we know we are welcomed into God's presence.

> Let us therefore draw near with confidence to the throne of grace, that we may receive mercy and may find grace to help in time of need. (Hebrews 4:16 NASB)
>
> Blessed be God, who has not turned away my prayer, nor His lovingkindness from me. (Psalm 66:20 NASB)

When we pray, we can call upon the Holy Spirit to guide our prayers.

> And in the same way the Spirit also helps our weakness; for we do not know how to pray as we should, but the Spirit Himself intercedes for us with groanings too deep for words; and He who searches the hearts knows what the mind of the Spirit is, because He intercedes for the saints according to the will of God. (Romans 8:26–27 NASB)
>
> Pray in the Spirit on all occasions with all kinds of prayers and requests. (Ephesians 6:18)

When we pray, we do so with confession, praise, and thanksgiving.

> If we confess our sins, he is faithful and just and will forgive us our sins and purify us from all unrighteousness. (1 John 1:9)
>
> Blessed be the God and Father of our Lord Jesus Christ, who has blessed us with every spiritual blessing in the heavenly places in Christ. (Ephesians 1:3 NASB)
>
> Always giving thanks to God the Father for everything. (Ephesians 5:20)
>
> Give thanks to the Lord, for he is good; his love endures forever! (Psalm 118:1)

One of the important principles of prayer is to rely upon the promises of God.

Ask and it will be given you; seek and you will find; knock and the door will be opened to you. (Matthew 7:7)

For the eyes of the Lord are upon the righteous, and his ears attend to their prayer. (1 Peter 3:12 NASB)

If we ask anything according to his will he hears us. And if we know that he hears us—whatever we ask—we know that we have what we asked of him. (1 John 5:14–15)

Know that the Lord has set apart the godly for himself; the Lord will hear when I call to him. (Psalm 4:3)

There may be times when you read a number of Bible passages with your friend to discover the truth of God's Word and to use a model for prayer right at that time.

For those who are suffering:

Blessed be the God and Father of our Lord Jesus Christ, who according to his great mercy has caused us to be born again to a living hope. . . . In this you greatly rejoice, even though now for a little while, if necessary, you have been distressed by various trials, that the proof of your faith, being more precious than gold which is perishable, even though tested by fire, may be found to result in praise and glory and honor at the revelation of Jesus Christ. (1 Peter 1:3, 6–7 NASB)

Do not be surprised at the fiery ordeal among you, which comes upon you for your testing . . . but to the degree that you share sufferings of Christ, keep on rejoicing, so that also at the revelation of His glory, you may rejoice with exultation. (1 Peter 4:12–13 NASB)

Consider it all joy, my brethren, when you encounter various trials, knowing that the testing of your faith produces endurance. (James 1:2–3 NASB)

For those who are worried:

Be anxious for nothing, but in everything by prayer and supplication with thanksgiving let your requests be made known to

God. And the peace of God, which passes all comprehension, shall guard your hearts and your minds in Christ Jesus. Finally, brethren, whatever is true, whatever is honorable, whatever is right, whatever is pure, whatever is lovely, whatever is of good repute, if there is any excellence and if anything worthy of praise, let your mind dwell on these things. The things you have learned and received and heard and seen in me, practice these things; and the God of peace shall be with you. (Philippians 4:6–9 NASB)

Do not fret because of evildoers, Be not envious toward wrongdoers. (Psalm 37:1 NASB)

For those who feel oppressed and in distress:

Answer me when I call, O God of my righteousness! Thou hast relieved me in my distress; Be gracious to me and hear my prayer. (Psalm 4:1 NASB)

My heart is in anguish within me, And the terrors of death have fallen upon me. Fear and trembling come upon me; And horror has overwhelmed me. And I say, "Oh that I had wings like a dove! I would fly away and be at rest. Behold, I would wander far away, I would lodge in the wilderness. I would hasten to my place of refuge From the stormy wind and tempest." . . . I shall call upon God, and the Lord will save me. Evening and morning and at noon, I will complain and murmur, and He will hear my voice. He will redeem my soul in peace from the battle which is against me, For they are many who strive with me. (Psalm 55:4–8, 16–18 NASB)

When I was in distress, I sought the Lord; at night I stretched out untiring hands and my soul refused to be comforted. I remembered you, O God, and I groaned; I mused, and my spirit grew faint. You kept my eyes from closing; I was too troubled to speak. I thought about the former days, the years of long ago; I remembered my songs in the night. My heart mused and my spirit inquired. . . . I will remember the deeds of the Lord; yes, I will remember your miracles of long ago. I will meditate on all your works and consider all your mighty deeds. (Psalm 77:2–6, 11–12)

Do not fear, for I have redeemed you; I have called you by name, you are Mine! When you pass through the waters, I will be with you; And through the rivers, they will not overflow you. When you walk through fire, you will not be scorched, Nor will the flame burn you. For I am the Lord your God, the Holy One of Israel, your Savior. (Isaiah 43:1–3 NASB)

For those who need God's forgiveness:

Who is a God like you, who pardons sin and forgives the transgression of the remnant of his inheritance? You do not stay angry forever but delight to show mercy. You will again have compassion on us; you will tread our sins underfoot and hurl all our iniquities into the depths of the sea. (Micah 7:18–19)

Then I acknowledged my sin to you and did not cover up my iniquity. I said, "I will confess my transgressions to the Lord"— and you forgave the guilt of my sin. (Psalm 32:5)

HOW TO PRAY

Over the years I've had numerous people tell me, "The only reason I'm here today was the knowledge that there was one person praying for me. That kept me going and gave me hope even when I felt hopeless."

Sometimes I would ask people exactly what they would like me to pray about and allow them to direct me. On other occasions I would say, "This is how I'm going to pray for you this week." There will be times when this is what keeps your friend going. And before you give this request to others or put it on a prayer chain, find out if this is all right with the other person. It's a way of also asking, "Whom do you want to know about this?"

As you pray, be sure to rely upon the Holy Spirit for instruction in how to pray. Allow the Holy Spirit to bring to mind through your imagination the direction needed in prayer. Too often we quickly pray with our own words, which come from our intellect. Our prayer lacks freshness because it reflects our own direction and not that of the Holy Spirit. It is as though we are uncomfortable with silence and feel that we must offer the right-sounding prayer. Too often our quick words block out the words the Holy Spirit wants to say to us.

Be careful in asking your friend to pray. He may be angry at God or just doesn't have the words at this time. "Grief has a way of plundering our prayer life, leaving us feeling immobile and empty."[1]

How then do you pray for your friend? Don't be intrusive with prayer. Ask your friend if he would like you to pray with him or for him. And don't pray long! Keep it brief but sensitive. And if you have the opportunity to pray for someone in the midst of deep difficulty, it is a privilege. I have seen some who pray because they either don't know what to say or they're uncomfortable with silence. I've seen some pray trying to fix or convict their friend. You pray to bring your friend to God and His resources.

The following are prayers to share with a friend:

O God, you are the Ruler of the universe, to you we commit our lives and trust in you for all our needs.

We don't understand the reason for the problems that we've experienced, nor do we need to. Our intent is to fully trust and fully accept the gifts you give as necessary and beneficial for us. Teach us to be thankful even when our immediate reaction is fear and distrust. Help us to be strong in our faith, to seek you, and in every circumstance to give thanks, as this is your will for our lives.

Finally, Father God, bring us at last into your presence, where all will be known to us as it has been known to you from before the beginning of time. Amen.[2]

Lord, we feel so alone and abandoned. I know you are still beside us, but help us to be more aware of your presence and what you might be trying to teach us through this crisis.

Protect us, and protect our children. Help us to forgive and to learn to be content—even in times of trial and tribulation.

I know that you desire good for us. Please guide and direct our paths. Amen.[3]

O Lord, we have experienced a great tragedy and wrong. We are suffering and grieving over our pain and loss. Please help us. Please come and comfort us in our heartache and grief. Give us wisdom to know how to help one another through this crisis. Give us strength to do the practical things that are necessary. Give us discernment to help each other in our personal and corporate suffering. Give us renewed faith to trust in you. And give us hope that we may be vessels of your goodness and mercy as we wait upon you. Amen.[4]

What's the best way to pray with your friends? Let me share what Dr. Gordon MacDonald suggested at a trauma conference in New York on how to pray for those in difficulty.

There are five kinds of prayers that your friends need as an intervention during their time of difficulty.

Give a *prayer of encouragement.*

Encourage means to press courage into a person. *Discourage* means to suck courage out of a person. Your hope, your courage, your belief in them and the future can be transferred to your friend. Ask for God to encourage your friend, to give him strength and courage. You might share with him how precious he is in God's sight. Read a Scripture such as Ephesians 1:4–6 to the person:

Long ago, even before he made the world, God loved us and chose us in Christ to be holy and without fault in his eyes. His unchanging plan has always been to adopt us into his own family by bringing us to himself through Jesus Christ. And this gave him great pleasure. So we praise God for the wonderful kindness he has poured out on us because we belong to his dearly loved Son. (NLT)

A prayer might be, "Oh God, my friend means so much to me and to you. I believe as you do that he has the ability and the strength to carry on in the midst of this difficulty. Give him a clear mind, a peaceful mind, and your guidance."

When a person questions whether or not God cares for him, I have shared portions of this song, an adaptation of Zephaniah 3:14, 17 and Psalm 54:2, 4:

And the Father will dance over you in joy!
He will take delight in whom He loves.
Is that a choir I hear singing the praises of God?
No, the Lord God Himself is exulting over you in song!
And He will joy over you in song!
My soul will make its boast in God,
For He has answered all my cries.
His faithfulness to me is as sure as the dawn of a new day.
Awake my soul, and sing!
Let my spirit rejoice in God!
Sing, O daughter of Zion, with all of your heart!
Cast away fear for you have been restored!
Put on the garment of praise as on a festival day.
Join with the Father in glorious, jubilant song.
God rejoices over you in song![5]

A prayer you could share might be:

Dear God, thank you for your act of choosing, adopting and making my friend your heir. Thank you that he is never out of your mind. Thank you for the never-ending joy you have over him. May he experience all of this at this moment in time.

Another prayer is the *prayer of restoration*. This is for the person who has failed or thinks he has failed. He has nothing left and is exhausted. Grief has overwhelmed him. He needs someone to pray and restore a sense of grace in his life. And he needs this often. His tank is empty and it needs to be filled. Perhaps it's as simple as "Lord, just fill my friend with hope for today and tomorrow. May he be secure in your arms," or "Lord, help my friend to know he is loved."

Gordon MacDonald prayed for a friend in this way:

> O Lord God, here's my friend whom I've come to love. You know how much he's hurting today, Lord. I know that he's fearful. I know that he's in physical pain. Lord, he needs something from you that no human being can give him. He needs new power in his life. He needs new courage in his life. He needs to know that tomorrow can be brighter than anything that's been in the past. Lord, he needs the kind of strength that only heaven can give. So, Lord, would you take my friend today? I put my hands on him so you know who he is. Would you take my friend today and bring healing to his broken life?[6]

A third kind of prayer is the *prayer of affirmation*. That's the prayer in which you recognize something in your friend that he cannot see in himself.

> Lord, I thank you for the way my friend is making such good decisions this past week and the way he continues to _____. We see what you are doing in his life.

When you pray a prayer of affirmation for your friend, when you pray before the Lord on behalf of your friend, you are building value and confidence that God wants him to have. In doing this you're a balcony person. You're leaning out of the balcony and saying, "Yes, you can do it. You're capable. See what you've already done. Wow!"

Be affirming in your comments and your prayers.

There is also a *prayer of blessing*, in which you pronounce upon another person what you know is God's purpose and will for him. It's also an act of one person verbally invoking God's gracious power in another's life. You find this within the Scriptures again and again.

> The Lord bless you and keep you; the Lord make his face shine upon you and be gracious to you; the Lord turn his face toward you and give you peace. (Numbers 6:24–26)

What could you say?

> Blessed be the God and Father of our Lord Jesus Christ. May He bless you with _____.
> May the Lord bless you and keep you strong. . . .
> May the Lord give you hope that will neither despair nor disappoint. . . .

Last is the *prayer of intercession.* This is called for when your friend is so weak and needy that you need to stand between him and God and pray the prayer that needs to be prayed on his behalf. In John 17 Jesus intercedes for His disciples. We are called to pray on our friend's behalf. And you will know what is needed as you listen to what your friend says to you.

You could pray the following:

> Lord Jesus, I pray the very words and thoughts of God for the protection of my friend. Please honor my prayers and surround my friend with your protection. Protect him from all evil. In the name of Jesus.

> Father, sometimes events intrude into our lives that bring distress and discouragement. Use your word and the work of your Holy Spirit to lift this from my friend and bring comfort. I thank you in advance for doing this. In Jesus' name I pray.

> Dear God, my friend needs the Holy Spirit as the Great Comforter at this moment to overcome the pain and distress.

Be simple in your prayers. Be short. Be sincere. And if you promise to pray, write yourself a reminder so you are faithful. Let your friend know that you've been praying.

You can never fully understand the power of prayer in your hurting friend's life.

Chapter 12

WHAT TO DO—WHAT NOT TO DO

I WOULD LIKE TO HELP. I really would. But I just don't know what to say. I'm sure I say too much and sometimes I think what I say hurts more than it helps. So, most of the time, I stay away and don't do anything at all."

One of your friends might come to you with a problem you've never encountered before. And you will wonder, *What should I say? How should I respond?*

As Christians, we have an opportunity to share Christ's love by the way we reach out to comfort and support others when they have endured a loss. But there are guidelines for us to follow in reacting to the grief of a friend or relative. A number of suggestions have already been given throughout this book. Some will be reiterated here because they are so important, and some new guidelines will be discussed as well.

HELPING THE TERMINALLY ILL

What if a friend discovers she is terminally ill? Most people find it hard to know what to say to a person who's been diagnosed as having a terminal illness. Often they say nothing, which makes them appear uncaring. If you have heard that your friend has a terminal illness, open your conversation by saying, "I understand you've been ill lately." *Then take your cues from the person.* If she wants to talk about it, she will. Tune in to her feelings and respond not just to what is said, but to the nonverbal communication as well. If she chooses not to discuss her illness, then it's her choice. At least you've acknowledged her illness and let her know you care about her.

"The ill person often thinks that friends are going to think less of them because they're ill. The patient thinks, 'They're going to see me undesirable as a friend.' People don't want to deal with it because they have to think about the possibility of their own death. They don't know what to say, so they avoid [saying anything]."[1]

Uncommon responses? No. Not knowing what to say is probably the most common and frustrating feeling we experience when a friend or loved one is going through a loss experience. We all struggle with what to say, how to say it, and when to respond. But it is possible to learn how to minister to others in a way that is supportive and caring.

You will need to acknowledge that the loss has occurred in this person's life and see it through her eyes rather than your own. There are some basic introductory questions you can use to show you care. "Would you like to tell me what happened? I'd like to hear about it." "What is each day like for you now?" "What's your greatest concern at this time?" "Tell me about your sleeping and eating."

THE "DO NOTS"

Four major "do nots" need to be followed: (1) Do not withdraw from the relative or friend. (2) Do not compare, evaluate, or judge the person or her responses. (3) Do not look for sympathy for yourself. (4) Do not patronize or pity the person.

In the case of any loss, a person needs continuing, ongoing support from a number of people. Often the support we give is out of proportion. When there is a death the bereaved friend is often inundated by people, calls, and cards. But two weeks later, she feels like a social outcast. Nobody calls, nobody writes. One woman remarked, "Few people call now. I'm very lonely. No one worries about my meals or how I am managing my time. People suddenly disappeared, assuming I'm fully recovered from my loss. I'm not recovered. My loneliness now seems even worse. I'm embarrassed that I miss feeling *special*."[2]

It's as though the whole world has gone merrily on its way, leaving the person alone. This creates a tremendous feeling of isolation. The bereaved individual needs comfort on a consistent basis. She needs to be able to talk about what has occurred and reminisce. For example, in both death and divorce there are major decisions that need to be made. In all types of loss a support group may be needed immediately. (See the recommendations at the end of the book.)

When you see your friend or relative, the most basic response is to ask how the person is doing and feeling. A simple, "How are you doing? It's been ten days since you lost _____. How are you feeling?" will open the door. The important thing then is to let the person talk without feeling that you're comparing, evaluating, or judging.

The third "do not" involves eliciting sympathy for yourself. It sounds strange, but it does happen. Some people talk more about their own sense of loss and grief in an effort to express their sorrow and empathy. But you cannot expect the other person to help you at this time. This is a time for you to give, not receive. If you need assistance, get it from somebody else.

Have you ever felt patronized by another person? You know what that feels like, don't you? You end up feeling dependent and childlike. You begin to wallow in self-pity and feel worse than before you interacted with the "helpful" person. Any kind of condescending response or behavior tends to reinforce the hurting feelings and basically shows that we really don't care as much as we say.

THE "DO'S"

There are several positive guidelines—or "do's"—to follow in ministering to a friend, relative, or neighbor. The first step is simply accepting what has happened and how she is responding. You may have your own perspective as to what your friend should be doing or how she should be responding, but you are not an authority on that individual's responses, so you will need to revise your expectations.

Accept her and let her know her feelings are normal. Some are going to apologize to you for their tears, their depression, or their anger. You will hear comments like, "I can't believe I'm still crying like this. I'm so sorry." "I don't know why I'm so upset. It was unfair letting me go like that, after fifteen years at that job. I know I shouldn't be angry, but I guess I really am."

You can be an encourager by accepting her feelings and the fact that she has feelings. Give her the gift of facing her feelings and expressing them. There are many statements that you can make to your friend:

"I don't want you to worry about crying in front of me. It's hard to feel this sad and not express it in tears. You may find me crying with you at times."

"I hope you feel the freedom to express your sorrow in tears in front of me. I won't be embarrassed or upset. I just want to be here with you."

"If I didn't see you cry, I would be more concerned. Your crying tells me you are handling this in a healthy way."

"If I had experienced what you have been through, I would feel like opening my eyes and letting the flood of tears come pouring out. Do you ever feel like that?"

Anger is another feeling that is difficult for many people to express. Use comments like:

"It is natural to feel anger and hostility toward everyone and everything that had to do with your husband's death. I feel angry too."

"You must be very angry that your baby has suffered and you can do nothing about it."

"It is normal and reasonable to be angry and resentful when you have lost your baby while others have live and healthy babies."

"You have lost your daughter and you have a right to be angry and frustrated."

"It must be hard to find the words to express your anger, helplessness, and frustration."

"It is important that you allow yourself to express your anger and rage no matter how much others try to discourage you."[3]

Your encouragement to express feelings will help the grieving person understand that her expression will not cause you to withdraw from her. Reassure her that you are not going to leave because of her feelings or try to talk her out of feeling the way she does. Your support is going to remain.

Another positive way of responding is with touch. But be sensitive to the person you're ministering to who may not be as comfortable with touch as you are. If she seems to reject your physical gestures such as hugs or a hand on the shoulder, be sure to respect her. If you extend a hand and she stiffens up, it's a good indication that your brief words and physical presence will help more than touch. In time she may come to you and say, "I need a hug."

Sometimes it helps just to say, "I'll be here in the house with you for a while. When you need me to leave or to do something for you, please let me know and I'll do it." Never assume she doesn't need you. Find out by talking with her.

Many people you minister to *will* need touch, since for many people, touching eases the emptiness of the inner pain. A widow expresses her feelings in this way:

Your mind is still on crutches. . . . There is something awe-inspiring, silencing, and shattering about emotional pain that does leave one at a loss for words. Perhaps gestures are better. I've mentioned before my need for hugs. I'm sure other people feel the same way. Human physical comfort, no strings. I saw a cartoon once, no caption. . . . It was [on a] vending machine; the sign on it read: "Hugs 25 cents." I wish I could have one installed.[4]

In his delightful book *Just a Touch of Nearness*, Fred Bauer tells this story:

I once heard about the tragic traffic death of a young child. Nancy, just six years old, had been struck by a speeding car. Her parents were devastated. So were her schoolmates, especially Joyce, Nancy's closest friend. As soon as Joyce heard the news about Nancy, she wanted to run to her friend's house. But Joyce's mother thought it would be too upsetting for their daughter and for Nancy's parents. "Daddy and you and I will go to the funeral," she consoled. "You can see Nancy's parents there." But a tearful Joyce insisted that she must see them immediately.

What worried Joyce's mother was what she herself might say to the grieving parents. But finally, reluctantly, she agreed to take her daughter to Nancy's house. And when they arrived, Joyce ran to her lost friend's mother, climbed up on her lap, and threw her arms around her. Wordlessly, the two of them cried out their mutual hurt.

No one who came to say, "I'm sorry," said it better than Joyce.[5]

THE GIFT OF LISTENING

One of the greatest gifts that you can give to a hurting, grieving person is the gift of listening, which I've already talked about. When people know you hear them, they will trust you and feel safe with you. And if you are a good listener, others will be more apt to invite you into their lives. Those you listen to will also learn through your example to respond openly and lovingly to what you share with them.

Nurturing listening is very important in helping your friend. In this type of listening, you listen for the emotional content behind the message being shared and reflect it to the speaker in an empathetic manner in your own words. Nurturing listening conveys support, caring, and acceptance for the person and his or her point of view. It extends a warm invitation to the griever to share his deepest joys, concerns, or hurts with you.

The following dialogue, one of the weekly telephone conversations between Frank and his father, illustrates this kind of listening. Frank's father and mother had been married for fifty-one years before she died nearly three years ago. Frank's father was deeply shaken by his loss and he still doesn't go out much. Many of his friends have encouraged him to continue his hobbies and to stay busy visiting his many grandchildren. Notice how Frank nurtures his father by simply listening and sharing empathetic responses:

Frank: Hi, Dad. How are you doing today?

Dad: I'm getting along just fine, son.

Frank: You're doing okay, then.

Dad: Yes, as well as I can with your mother gone.

Frank: Dad, it sounds as if you still feel Mom's passing deeply. It was a real loss.

Dad: You know, I didn't think it was going to be this bad. I didn't think it would take this long to recover.

Frank: After all the years you were together, you miss her and miss the times you had together.

Dad *(after a pause, with a slight break in his voice)*: Frank, I miss her each day, and sometimes I feel lonely all day long. Lots of friends want me to move on with life and not think about her so much. But I want to remember. There are so many good memories.

Frank: You sound as if you want to do something to help you remember Mom.

Dad: This may sound dumb, but I really want to go visit some of the places Mom and I used to go together. I was thinking about taking one or two of the grandkids with me. What do you think?[6]

Did Frank give his opinion of what his father ought to do? Did he advise his father on a decision? Did he try to cheer up his father? No. He simply listened reflectively in a way that nurtured his father and encouraged him to express his inner thoughts and feelings. Frank's responses made his dad feel understood. That's what people want: someone who understands and accepts them. As you learn to nurture others with your listening, you can fill their need for understanding and acceptance.

As you listen you are going to hear the same thoughts expressed again and again. Grieving people, whether it be the loss of a pet, a job, a home, a pregnancy, or a person, have a compelling need to retell the details of their loss. They want to talk about the who, what, when, and how. The details vary depending on the nature of the loss. Do you remember why a person tends to focus so much on the details, and in some cases, final conversations with someone they lost? It gives her an opportunity to hold on to whatever she lost. Don't be put off by the details of the story even though you may know them by heart. This telling of details goes on for three or four months until she is assured that she will not lose the memory of the person she lost. When she reaches that point, the clinging to exacting details will lessen. She will begin to let go.

When grieving people give the details, encourage them to express the accompanying feelings as well. Their feelings will be relieved as you listen without shock, embarrassment, or judgment.

Often in the case of an accident, loss of an important position, or death you will hear the person taking responsibility for what occurred even when she had no responsibility or could not have done anything about what happened. This is an opportunity for you to say something like: "What could you really have done to prevent that from happening? Would that really have been possible? Is there anyone else who could have done anything? If so, why didn't they? I can see how you might feel that way, but there really was nothing that any of us could have done." Before you make statements such as these, help them identify all of their "if only" and "regret" statements they may have.

Above all, don't say too much to the hurting person. Your presence speaks volumes. Joseph Bayly wrote a book many years ago called *The Last Thing We Talk About.* It is the story of how he and his wife coped with the deaths of three of their sons. He gave this advice:

> Sensitivity in the presence of grief should usually make us more silent, more listening. "I'm sorry" is honest; "I know how you feel" is usually not—even though you may have experienced the death of a person who had the same familial relationship to you as the deceased person had to the grieving one. If the person feels that you can understand, he'll tell you. Then you may want to share your own honest, not prettied-up feelings in your personal aftermath with death. Don't try to "prove" anything to a survivor. An arm around the shoulder, a firm grip of the hand, a kiss: these are the proofs grief needs, not logical reasoning. I was sitting, torn by grief. Someone came and talked to me of God's dealings, of why it happened, of hope beyond the grave. He talked constantly, he said things I knew were true. I was unmoved, except to wish he would go away. He finally did. Another came and sat beside me. He didn't ask leading questions. He just sat beside me for an hour and more, listened when I said something, answered briefly, prayed simply, left, I was moved. I was comforted. I hated to see him go.[7]

PATIENCE: A NECESSARY CHARACTER QUALITY

If there is one character quality that is necessary in ministering to a grieving person, it is patience. You will hear the same story, same details, and see the same tears again and again. This is normal. It's necessary. What may be quite uncomfortable for you is anger. The extent of the person's anger may cause you to want to say, "Enough!" but it's a natural healthy response if it is within reasonable bounds.

You may even become the target for your friend's anger. If she withdraws, don't push her. This is part of grief. It's as though she moves in and out of the real world. She will progress at her pace, not yours. The author of *Beyond Grief* describes the process so well:

> No schedule exists for healing. A survivor is raw with grief and must endure much pain before healing takes place. The only course you can take is to avoid appearing restless or annoyed with the survivor.
>
> It may be difficult for you to achieve a balance between *acknowledging the loss* that caused the survivor pain, and *maintaining proper perspective* in the face of that loss. You cannot help the survivor by blocking reality or steering a survivor away from painful reminders of the loss, but at the same time, you need to maintain a positive perspective while facilitating grief.
>
> You can do this by validating the person who died, talking about how the person touched or enriched the lives of other people. When the opportunity arises, mention facets of life in which the survivor has formerly shown interest. Make a mental list of those activities or people who gave the survivor enjoyment. Keep the sparks of those natural interests alive or at least present, by mentioning them—the garden, the pets, the survivor's favorite shopping area, golf partner, or community interest. By doing this you are indicating to the survivor that *there has been a past* and *there will be a future* with these same things, people and places in it.[8]

PRACTICAL HELP

There are also many practical things you can do to help, regardless of the type of loss. I hope you will begin to respond to all of the losses people experience, some of which don't have much social recognition or support. Any major loss cuts very deep, whether it is divorce, personal rejection, job loss, or death.

With each loss you will need to (1) discover your friend's personal situation and needs; (2) decide what you are willing and able to do for her, realizing that you can neither do it all, nor should you; and (3) contact her and offer to do the most difficult of the jobs you've chosen. If your friend rejects your offer, suggest another. Specific tasks could include feeding pets, making and delivering meals, doing yard work, making difficult phone calls, obtaining needed information regarding support groups or new employment, providing transportation, being available to run errands, and so forth. At some point in time, giving her a sensitive, supportive book on loss and grief could be helpful.[9]

If the loss affected one person, minister to that person. But if it affected the family unit, there needs to be a ministry to each family member, both adults and children. Be sensitive to all members of the family. I've heard many husbands say, "I'm so tired of people asking how my wife is doing. For once I wish they'd ask how I'm doing." Discover which of their social involvements will be the most difficult for them and be available for support.

As each year goes by, friends and relatives lose loved ones. Prior to Christmas, we look over the Christmas card list to make sure we have made proper changes so the name on the card doesn't upset the recipient. For a widow, receiving cards still addressed to "Mr. and Mrs." can be painful.

In deciding how you can minister to others, you will find a set of helpful guidelines in *What to Say When You Don't Know What to Say* by Lauren Briggs. I would encourage you to read this section over again and again so it will truly be yours when you need to reach out and minister to another person. This is the best summary of guidelines I've found:

What Not to Do

Don't try to minimize your friend's pain with comments like, "It's probably for the best." "Things could be worse." "You'll remarry." "You're young, you can always have another one." "You're strong, you'll get over it soon." "You know God is in control." Comments like these might be an attempt to offer hope, but to a hurting person, they sound as though you don't comprehend the enormity of what's happened. These don't acknowledge their pain and loss.

What It's Best to Do

You can offer simple, understanding statements such as: "I feel for you during this difficult time." "This must be very hard for you." "I share your feelings of loss." "I wish I could take the hurt away." Comments like these let the person know you acknowledge their pain and it's okay for them to feel that way.

What Not to Do

Don't say, "I'm so sorry," and end the sentence. Your hurting friend is probably sorry too, but he can't respond to that kind of comment.

What It's Best to Do

Say, "I'm so sorry." Then add, "I know how special he was to you." "I'll miss her also." "I want to help you; I'm available any time you need me." "I've been praying for you. Is there something specific I should be praying for?"

What Not to Do

Don't just say, "Is there anything I can do to help?"

What It's Best to Do

Be aggressive with your willingness to help. Ask yourself, "What would I need if I were in a similar situation?" Offer specific things you can do for her, like, "I'm on my way to the store. What can I pick up for you?" "Would tomorrow be a good day to help you with the laundry?" "Would your children like to come over and play this afternoon?" Most of the time, a person in a crisis can't decide what she does need. Besides, she probably doesn't want to impose.

What Not to Do

Don't say, "You shouldn't feel that way."

What It's Best to Do

Encourage her to keep a journal or write down her thoughts and feelings. Often, just seeing her thoughts on paper helps her deal with what she is facing.

What Not to Do

Do not try to answer her questions of "Why?" You don't have any answer and at this time even the true answer may not be apparent. Job's friends didn't help with their responses, and Job said, "Miserable comforters are you all!" (Job 16:2).

What It's Best to Do

Simply answer, "I don't know why. I guess both of us would like to have some answers at this time. You would especially. I wish I had an answer to give you."

What Not to Do

Don't offer spiritual answers as to why she's facing this problem or tell her that she'll be a stronger person afterward. We don't know why tragedies happen—why certain people have to go through such trauma.

What It's Best to Do

Agree when she expresses her feelings. Say, "Yes, what happened to you isn't fair and doesn't make any sense," whether or not you share the same perspective.

What Not to Do

Don't put timetables on your hurting friend's recovery. Your inference that she's not coping well or should be her old self by now only hinders her progress. Everyone is different and recovery varies.

What It's Best to Do

Allow her all the time she needs to deal effectively with all the phases of her grief.

What Not to Do

Don't quote Bible verses as a way to correct or minimize someone's feelings. Think very carefully, asking yourself if a passage will communicate comfort or condemnation. Never offer spiritual suggestions from a position of superiority or self-righteousness.

What It's Best to Do

Give spiritual encouragement from your heart, and include Bible verses that have comforted you at a difficult time. Let her know you will pray for her daily. If you pray with her, keep it brief, reflecting her feelings in the prayer and focusing upon God's understanding of her pain and the fact that He will be her source of comfort.

What Not to Do

Don't say "I understand" when you haven't faced the same situation. Telling someone that everything will be all right when you have never known the depth of her hardship is an empty statement. And she doesn't need to hear horror stories of people you know who have been through something similar.

What It's Best to Do

Be honest about your experiences. If you haven't endured her particular kind of tragedy, say, "I haven't been through what you're facing, but I want you to know I care about you and will support you through the difficult time ahead." If you've had a similar crisis, tell her about it briefly, adding that you can empathize with her feelings. Of course, you can't completely understand because you haven't been through the past experiences that laid the foundation for their reaction.

What Not to Do

Don't ignore her needs after the immediate loss has subsided.

What It's Best to Do

Keep in touch for months, especially at the critical times discussed in this book, letting her know you're praying for her. Ask how she's really doing and send thoughtful notes with encouraging words.

What Not to Do

Don't expect unrealistic optimism or levity from your hurting friend.

What It's Best to Do

Realize that her heart is full of pain and turmoil. Let her know that you will listen to her feelings and want to be part of that pain.

What Not to Do

Don't offer clichés or be unrealistically optimistic to cover up your insecurities.

What It's Best to Do

Indicate your love by saying, "I really feel awkward because I'm not sure what to say, what you need, or how to help you, but I want you to know that I love you. I'm praying for you and I'm available."

What Not to Do

Don't use "shoulds" or "if onlys" such as: "You should give the clothes away." "You should go back to work and get over this." "You should have more faith." "If only you had watched him more carefully." "If only you hadn't been so strict." "If only you ate better."

What It's Best to Do

Allow hurting people to make the decisions and take the necessary steps to deal with the trauma. No one can tell another how they should feel.

What Not to Do

Don't offer unasked-for advice. If your suggestions weren't solicited they may not be appreciated.

What It's Best to Do

Respond cautiously and prayerfully with uplifting and edifying ideas when your friend asks for your help. Let her know that you pray for her daily. On occasion, ask how she would like you to be praying for her.[10]

Be careful in ever saying, "This must be God's will." Rather, let your friend know that God is present with her in this suffering even if she doesn't sense Him, and He is the Comforter and Protector in the midst of pain and tragedy. But be sensitive as to when you share this.

As you have walked through your own losses, you will be better able to help others walk through their valleys of loss. The walk can be so lonely when it is undertaken alone. But when others come along to just be there, listen, weep, and comfort through their presence, grievers are sustained.

None of us walks alone. Jesus Christ has been there and He is with us all of the time to sustain, encourage, and support us. Yes, life is full of losses, but Jesus Christ makes it possible to conquer them.

Grief Support Groups

IDEALLY YOUR CHURCH will have an ongoing grief recovery group. Even very small churches have found it possible to develop this type of ministry to minister to their congregations as well as the needs of the community.

GriefShare is a program established in churches across the United States. This material provides resources for a thirteen-week grief recovery seminar/support group. A church is equipped with a video session for each meeting, a leader's guide, leader-equipping video, and workbooks for group participants. Qualified lay people can lead this program. All the content needed is within the material. GriefShare videos feature interviews with thirty leading authors, speakers, counselors, and pastors with broad expertise in grief recovery from a biblical Christ-centered perspective. For information on establishing a support group in your church or finding an existing one call 1-800-875-7560 or go to *www.hnormanwright.com.*

Divorce care is a similar type of program with videos and workbooks. Call 1-800-875-7560.

ADDITIONAL SUPPORT GROUP ORGANIZATIONS:

Compassionate Friends (For parents who have lost children)
www.compassionatefriends.org
P.O. Box 3696
Oakbrook, IL 60522-3696
708-990-0010

Parents of Murdered Children
www.pomc.com
100 E. 8th St. Room 341

Cincinnati, OH 45202
513-721-5683
513-345-4489 (fax)

The Tragedy Assistance Program for Survivors (TAPS) (Provides help for those who lose family members to military deaths)
www.taps.org
2001 S Street, NW, #300
Washington, DC 20009
1-800-959-TAPS
202-639-5312 (fax)

TAG: Teen Age Grief, Inc. (Provides training and resources to help grieving teens)
www.smartlink.net/~tag
P.O. Box 220034
Newhall, CA 91322-0034
1-805-253-1932

The National Hospice Organization (For information on locating hospice services in your area, click on Find a Program)
www.nhpco.org
1901 North Moore Street, Suite 901
Arlington, VA 22209
1-800-658-8898 (help line)

ENDNOTES

Chapter 1

1. Harold Ivan Smith, *When You Don't Know What to Say* (Kansas City, MO: Beacon Hill Press, 2002), 15.
2. Nina Herrmann Donnelley, *I Never Know What to Say* (New York: Ballantine Books, 1987), 21–22.
3. Ibid., adapted, 17–24.
4. Smith, *When You Don't Know What to Say*, 7.

Chapter 2

1. Frederick Buechner, *Peculiar Treasures: A Biblical Who's Who* (New York: Harper & Row, 1979), 65.
2. As quoted in Bob Diets, *Life After Loss* (Tucson, AZ: Fisher Books, 1988), 148.
3. Charlotte E. Thompson, *Raising a Handicapped Child* (New York: Morrow, 1986), adapted, 38–41.
4. Mary Ann Froehlich and PeggySue Wells, *What to Do When You Don't Know What to Say* (Minneapolis, MN: Bethany House, 2000), 98–99.
5. Ibid., 97–98.
6. Ibid., 96–97.
7. Ibid., 95.
8. Ibid., 94.
9. Betty Jane Wylie, *The Survival Guide for Widows* (New York: Ballantine Books, 1982), 115.
10. Michele McBride, *The Fire That Will Not Die* (Palm Springs, CA: ETC Publications, 1979), 154, 147, ix.
11. "Seeing With God's Eyes," *Today's Christian Woman* (March/April 1986), 31.
12. Source unknown.
13. Erin Linn, *I Know Just How You Feel: Avoid the Clichés of Grief* (Cary, IL: Publishers Mark, 1986), xii-xiii.
14. Written by Rita Moran, *Compassionate Friends* newsletter.

Chapter 3

1. Harold Kushner, *Living a Life That Matters*, 123–124. Quoted in Harold Ivan Smith, *When You Don't Know What to Say* (Kansas City, MO: Beacon Hill Press, 2002), 11.
2. Smith, *When You Don't Know What to Say*, 87.

Chapter 4

1. Dr. Ronald W. Ramsay and Rene Noorbergen, *Living With Loss* (New York: William Morrow and Co., Inc., 1981), adapted, 47–48.
2. Therese A. Rando, *Grieving: How to Go on Living When Someone You Love Dies* (Lexington, MA: Lexington Books, 1988), adapted, 556–557.
3. Ibid., 44.
4. Therese A. Rando, *Treatment of Complicated Mourning* (Champaign, IL: Research Press, 1983), 512.
5. Glen W. Davidson, *Understanding Mourning* (Minneapolis: Augsburg Publishing House, 1984), 59.
6. Ibid.
7. H. Norman Wright, *Will My Life Ever Be the Same?* (Eugene, OR: Harvest House, 2002), 100.

Chapter 5

1. Adapted from Ralph Hirschowitz, Addendum, "A Special Feature of the Levinson Letter" (Cambridge: The Levinson Institute, n.d.) 4, as found in Ahlem, *Living With Stress* (Ventura, Calif.: Regal, 1978).
2. Source unknown.
3. Charles Swindoll, *Growing Strong in the Seasons of Life* (Portland, OR: Multnomah, 1983), 274–275.
4. H. Norman Wright, *Crisis Counseling* (Ventura, CA: Regal Books, 1993), adapted from chapter 1.

Chapter 6

1. Donald Meichenbaum, *A Clinical Handbook/Practical: Therapist Manual for Assessing and Treating Adults With Post Traumatic Stress Disorder (PTSD)* (Waterloo, Ont.: Institute Press, 1994), adapted, 23.
2. Sandra L. Brown, *Counseling Victims of Violence* (Alexandria, VA: American Association for Counseling and Development, 1991), adapted, 9.
3. Diane Langberg, quoted from a presentation for the TRIP Conference, New York City, Oct. 2001, adapted.

4. Aphrodite Matsakis, *I Can't Get Over It: A Handbook for Trauma Survivors* (Oakland, CA: New Harbinger, 1992), adapted, 6–7.

5. Ibid., adapted, 23–24.

6. Ibid., adapted, 10–13.

Chapter 7

1. Diane Langberg, quoted from a presentation for the TRIP Conference, New York City, Oct. 2001, adapted.

2. Sandra L. Brown, *Counseling Victims of Violence* (Alexandria, VA: American Association for Counseling and Development, 1991), adapted, 22–24.

3. Robert Hicks, *Failure to Scream* (Grand Rapids, Mich.: Baker, 1996), adapted, p. 46.

4. Raymond B. Flannery, Jr., *Post-Traumatic Stress Disorder* (New York: Crossroad, 1992), adapted, 36–37.

5. Terence Monmaney, "For Most Trauma Victims Life Is More Meaningful," *L.A. Times*, Sunday Oct. 7, 2001, 9. Citing research from Richard Tedeschi, University of North Carolina; Dr. Robert Ursano, Uniformed Services University of the Health Sciences in Bethesda, MD; Dr. Sandra Bloom.

6. Matsakis, *I Can't Get Over It!* adapted, 134.

7. Ibid., adapted, 15, 153.

8. Ibid., adapted, 159.

9. Ibid., adapted, 160–163.

10. Ibid., adapted, 236.

11. H. Norman Wright, *Will My Life Ever Be the Same?* (Eugene, OR: Harvest House, 2002), adapted, chapter 8.

Chapter 8

1. Karl A. Slaikeu, *Crisis Intervention: A Handbook for Practice and Research* (Boston: Allyn and Bacon, 1984), adapted, 89–90.

2. H. Norman Wright, Baker Books, 1985.

3. H. Norman Wright, Harvest House, 1998.

4. Slaikeu, *Crisis Intervention*, 90–91.

Chapter 9

1. Richard F. Berg and Christine McCartney, *Depression and the Integrated Life* (New York: Alta House, 1981), 27.

2. Mitch Golant, Ph.D., and Susan K. Golant, *What to Do When Someone You Love Is Depressed* (New York: Henry Holt and Co., 1996), adapted, 90–92.

3. H. Norman Wright, *Winning Over Emotions* (Eugene, OR: Harvest House, 1998), 32–33.
4. Ibid., 36.

Chapter 10

1. Leonard M. Zunin, M.D., and Hilary Stanton Zunin, *The Art of Condolence* (New York: HarperCollins, 1991), adapted, 35–39.
2. Ibid., 38.
3. Robert V. Ozment, *When Sorrow Comes* (Waco, TX: Word Books, 1970), 50.
4. Barbara Russell Chesser, *Because You Care* (Waco, TX: Word Books, 1987), 119.
5. Norman Vincent Peale, *Wonderful Promises* (Carmel, NY: Guideposts, 1983), 32.
6. Phyllis Hobe, *Coping* (Carmel, NY: Guideposts, 1983), 233.
7. Chesser, *Because You Care*, 122–126.
8. Zunin and Zunin, *The Art of Condolence*, 61–62.
9. Ibid., 72–73.
10. Ibid., 97–98.

Chapter 11

1. J. Rupp, *Praying Our Goodbyes* (Notre Dame, IN: Ave Maria Press, 1988), 79.
2. Lisa Barnes Lampman, ed., *Helping a Neighbor in Crisis* (Wheaton, IL: Tyndale House, 1997), adapted, 67.
3. Ibid., adapted, 40.
4. Ibid., adapted, 68.
5. "And the Father Will Dance." Lyrics adapted from Zephaniah 3:14, 17 and Psalm 54:2, 4. Arranged by Mark Hayes. Used by permission.
6. MacDonald, Dr. Gordon. Trauma conference in New York, 2001.

Chapter 12

1. Source unknown.
2. Judy Tatelbaum, *The Courage to Grieve* (New York: Harper & Row, 1980), 44.
3. Donna Ewy and Rodger Ewy, *Death of a Dream* (New York: Dutton, 1984), adapted, 80.
4. Wylie, *Survival Guide for Widows*, 113.

5. Fred Bauer, *Just a Touch of Nearness* (Norwalk, CT: C.R. Gibson Co., 1985), 24–25.

6. Source unknown.

7. Joseph Bayly, *The Last Thing We Talk About* [formerly titled *The View from the Hearse*] (Colorado Springs, CO: Cook Communications, 1969, 1992), 40.

8. Carol Staudacher, *Beyond Grief* (Oakland, CA: New Harbinger Publications, 1987), 230–231.

9. Ibid., adapted, 231–232.

10. Lauren Briggs, *What to Say When You Don't Know What to Say* (Eugene, OR: Harvest House Publishers, 1985), adapted, 150–155.

H. NORMAN WRIGHT, the author of over seventy books, including *That's a Keeper* and *The Complete Book of Christian Wedding Vows*, is a licensed marriage, family, and child therapist and also a certified trauma specialist. He has taught at the graduate level at both Biola University and Talbot Seminary and is the founder and director of Christian Marriage Enrichment. Norm and his wife, Joyce, have been married for over forty years and make their home in Bakersfield, California.

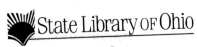